Dedicated to my daughters Courtney and Katie

and, as with anything and everything I do,

to my husband, Jim

1854: Revenge Comes with a Cost: The Death of James and Francis Wickham

Long before Lizzie Borden famously reduced the population of Fall River, Massachusetts, another husband and wife, right here on Long Island, were killed by an axe wielding psychopath in a heinous act of revenge.

James and Frances Wickham, after having sold their successful grocery, retired to a family owned farm in Cutchogue. They were aided by two young household servants, Ellen Howard and Catherine Dowd, a young black man named Stephen Winston, and an Irish farmhand, Nicholas Bain.

Nicholas Bain was an enormous black-haired man with an undulating walk. By 1854, he had worked for the Wickham's for three years. He had a drinking problem and was known to make amorous advances to all the local maids, especially Ellen Howard. When he asked her to marry him and was rejected, he became furious.

James and Nicholas argued often, sometimes about his drinking, other times about his harassment of Ellen. But the arguments never got to the point where James fired Nicholas. It was as true then as it is now: good help is hard to find.

But by May 31, 1854, James finally had had enough of Nicholas's inappropriate behavior and fired him. But even after being fired, Nicholas just wouldn't go away. He hung around the house, just to harass Ellen. By June 2nd, James had his fill of Nicholas and evicted him from the farm, telling him to never set foot there again.

While walking the 10 miles to the Greenport railroad station, Nicholas could be heard screaming that he was going to have his revenge. How dare James tell him what to do; how dare James kick him out? Having worked himself into a frenzy, Nicholas then turned around and walked the 10 miles back to the Wickham farm where he ransacked the barn for just the right weapon to get his revenge. He found it--an axe.

A short while later, Nicholas went to work getting his revenge. The two servant girls clung to each other while they listened to the sounds of Mr. Wickham being beaten and Mrs. Wickham screaming, "Nicholas, don't kill him, don't kill him." They shivered at the sound and knew that Nicholas would soon come looking for them. They had to get out of there.

Ellen and Catherine managed to escape their second story bedroom through a window and over the roof to the milk house where they finally saw an opportunity to jump down and run to a neighbors'. At first, the arrival of the two disheveled women in the middle of the night frightened the neighbor's wife, so she told her husband to turn them away, but the neighbor recognized the girls and opened the door, leading to the calling to arms of all the local men

When the cry quickly went out, Joseph Corwin, William Betts, and Dr. Carpenter rushed to the farm to see what was happening. They found James Wickham with 20 wounds; he also had his jaw broken in three places and his skull smashed. Yet, he wouldn't die for 20 more hours. Francis was found with similar wounds, but she wouldn't survive the night. The final victim was found in the kitchen, the young man who worked on the farm, Stephen Winston. His ear had been severed and his skull fractured. He would die the next day.

Nicholas had not only left his hat behind, but there were large bloody footprints, which would make following the killer very easy, you would think, but it would take a few more days to get him in custody. There had not been a murder in Southold in 30 years, and no one in the community had ever participated in a manhunt like that.

Hundreds of men joined in the search. They were going to make sure Nicholas Bain was caught and properly punished. If Nicholas had been a smarter killer, he might have gotten away with it in this community. But, sadly for him, he was not.

Bain was seen at a neighboring house begging for food. When he returned the next morning, hungry again, the farmer finally recognized him and asked him "you are the man who has done these murders?" Remember this is prior to daily home delivered newspapers, television, or the Internet, so this man can be forgiven for it taking him so long to recognize a killer who had been identified on the night of the murder.

The response of "I did not do as much as I meant to" convinced the farmer he had the right man, so he attempted to apprehend him on his own. This didn't work out so well and Bain got away.

The men searched tirelessly through the thick woods, and on the day of the Wickham's funeral, they finally tracked Nicholas down near the train tracks. There he sat with the blood of his victims soaked through his pant legs; a shallow two-inch self-inflicted wound on his neck, a feeble suicide attempt. The men grabbed him and were ready to string him up then and there.

Were it not for the level head of the sheriff, that would have happened. But Nicholas was incarcerated in the Riverhead jail, tried and convicted of first degree murder. Emotions were running high on the day of the execution. The authorities felt it necessary to enlist the aid of the local militia to maintain order in the courtyard behind the jail where the gallows had been erected. Bain paid for his crimes with thousands of people watching and cheering.

1872: Tarred and Feathered: The Demise of Charles Kelsey

On August 29, 1873, local fishermen experienced the catch of a lifetime when they pulled the lower half of Charles G. Kelsey's body from Cold Spring Harbor. The mystery of Kelsey's disappearance was now solved. But another took its place: Who killed Charles Kelsey? An ill-trained magician perhaps?

Charles was a wealthy Huntington farmer, poet, and educator, who spoke three languages and was a local authority on literature. All this made him stand out among the other men in town, but not in a good way. Those men were farmers and laborers who worked with their hands and couldn't quite "get" Charles. What kind of man would rather sit in his house writing poetry instead of hunting or fishing? But the women of the town did see the allure in

Charles; they saw him as a romantic figure and their husbands, fathers, and brothers as heathens.

While teaching Sunday school, Charles met Julia Smith who reportedly had been one of his Sunday-school pupils and 10 years his junior. A clandestine affair ensued. This made him a target for the men who saw his interest in Julia as inappropriate and questioned why she would be interested in a man like Charles when there were perfectly good men available who were "real" men?

Julia Smith lived in Huntington with her wealthy grandmother, Charlotte Oakley. Mrs. Oakley disapproved of her granddaughter's affections for Charles for obvious reasons, so the lovers had to meet in secret. Julia would leave a lantern burning in the basement window to signal that the coast was clear, all very romantic for the young Julia. Julia soon tired of this relationship. What fun was it to have a boyfriend you couldn't tell anyone about? She started seeing Samuel Sammis, someone closer in age, with whom she could be seen. Kelsey did not react well to being dumped for a younger man and published nasty poetry about her in the local paper, an action that quite possibly cost him his life.

On November 3rd, 1872, Charles was returning from a political rally celebrating Grant's victory over Horace Greeley when he noticed Julia's signal burning in the basement window. He had seen this same signal the night before, but when he slipped into Julia's bedroom window, her aunt was in the bed instead of Julia, so Charles fled. So, this time, should he take the bait?

Drawn to this beacon as a moth to a flame, Charles' fate was similarly sealed. Assuming she had changed her mind and wanted him back, he approached the bedroom window. But Julia had been persuaded to entice Charles to the yard where a group of masked men were waiting in the bushes prepared to teach him a lesson.

The men seized him, stripped Charles of all his clothes, and cut off his hair and beard. At some point, Charles must have noticed the large pail of tar and bags of feathers and knew what was coming. The men first coated him with the hot tar that blistered his skin and caused excruciating pain and then covered him with feathers. The tar was for pain and the feathers for humiliation. Tar and feathering was a demeaning form of punishment, but not intended to kill. It burned the skin going on and can be even more painful when removed. This activity alone was not, obviously, meant to kill him, so how did he end up dead?

After this ordeal, Charles was paraded in front of his young lover and her grandmother, then in front of the neighborhood wives to humiliate him even further and show the wives that he was just a silly man who preferred little girls to a real woman. What happened next is a mystery that lingers today.

Charles' sister found a tar-covered watch in Charles' kitchen and signs of a struggle in the yard - evidence that he had arrived home that evening after his humiliation. But there was no sign of Charles until half of him, from the waist down, surfaced 10 months later in the harbor. Doctors who inspected the body testified that it had been savagely mutilated and then weighted down at the waist with ropes, which eventually severed it in two. So it seemed the most gruesome aspect of this crime was not intentional.

A funeral was held for what was left of Charles. Although the townspeople's feelings over his death varied, no one would have missed this funeral for anything. Early on the day of the funeral, a sign was tacked to the door of the general store. It read, "Funeral of the Legs!"

But the pastor wouldn't allow Charles' casket to be brought into the packed church, so it was left on the front lawn.

Across the country, Huntington became known as "Tar Town." Calling it a place of "abominable women, fiendish men and imbecile officers," a local newspaper claimed Huntington had "blotted the history of Long Island with an outrage of which the cutthroats of Missouri would have been ashamed."

As for Julia Smith, she married Royal Sammis three months before Charles' remains were discovered. Though her husband and another local man were indicted for murder in the second degree, they were never tried. No one was ever convicted of Charles Kelsey's murder. The mystery of who killed him continues and a plaque commemorating the event still stands in Huntington today, reminding the town that at one time the good people of Huntington were more interested in revenge than art and culture.

1887-- Mother Knows Best: Cynthia Hawkins

To some mothers, no girl will ever be good enough for their sons. In particular, the contempt Cynthia Hawkins bore for her son's love interests came at a heavy price – she paid with her life.

Cynthia was married to the wealthy Captain Franklin Hawkins. They, with their son, Francis, lived in Islip. During their son's teens, Cynthia and Franklin thought that Francis was exhibiting a disturbing attraction to the area shop girls and maids. This frightened Cynthia. What if one of these women got pregnant and trapped her son into marriage? That would not do at all. Her son was going to marry who she told him to marry, not some floosy.

The Captain's demise removed the family's male role model, and Cynthia was left to deal with her problem son alone. Cynthia, determined not to use her wealth to spoil her son and to assuage both of her concerns, sent

Francis to work at his uncle's grocery store in Bay Shore.

There, Mrs. Hawkins reasoned, under the watchful eye of

his uncle, Francis would be safe from these women's

clutches, and earn an honest $10 a week. Needless to say,

being deprived of his working class female friends and not

being allowed to share in the family's wealth irritated

Francis.

But mother's plan soon went awry. Francis met

Hattie Schreck, a young woman who worked in the soda

shop down the street from his uncle's grocery store. Before

long, they had become very close and young Francis

proposed marriage. Mrs. Hawkins was furious and forbid

Francis from seeing Hattie ever again.

Thus started a psychological tug of war. Francis'

mother and her money pulling in one direction and Hattie,

insisting they marry to prevent tarnishing her reputation,

pulling in the other direction. What was he to do?

Francis' temporary solution was a compromise: on Sundays he rented a buggy and paid a brief visit to his mother then spent the rest of the day in Northport with Hattie. But he needed a more permanent solution. Francis finally came up with the perfect and very permanent solution to his dilemma.

On October 2nd, 1887, Francis arrived at his mother's house with news that her sister was sick and needed Cynthia's help. During the drive, the two began to argue about Hattie. Francis could not convince his mother that the affection he felt was true love, and he wanted to get married. His mother did not understand why he had to marry her and ruin the reputation of the family. His mother continued her diatribe about his fiancé, causing Francis to lose his temper. Not being able to get his mother to change her mind, the decision was mad; if mother was going to continue to be unreasonable, Francis would have to take her out of the conversation. He took out the gun hidden in his coat pocket and shot his mother in the head then bludgeoned her with the butt of the gun. Cynthia's lifeless body was rolled out of the buggy and left by the side of the road and the murder weapon tossed into a nearby pond. His next movements proved this was not a fully baked plan.

Francis returned the blood soaked buggy and reserved it again for the next day. I guess Francis didn't think anyone would notice the blood dripping from the carriage, and he had had an exhausting day and just wanted to go to sleep. He would deal with it tomorrow. He picked up the buggy the next day, drove to Hattie's in Northport, and scrubbed the buggy clean, but it was too late. The buggy owner had found a large blood stain on the floor under where the buggy had been overnight and noticed blood stains on the seat before Francis took it out again. He contacted the police who were waiting for Francis when he returned the buggy. When the police searched Francis' bedroom, they found the blood soaked clothes he had worn the day before.

After his arrest, Francis continually proclaimed his innocence. But this self-serving statement did nothing to quell the mob bent on stringing him up outside the police station. Along the route to the jail, Francis and his captors passed the house where his mother's body reposed; Francis began to sing Climbing up the Golden Stairs. In April 1888, Francis was tried, convicted, and sentenced to hang.

In Suffolk County, no one had been hanged in 30 years. The hanging tree was being stored in the court house basement. It was resurrected, and on a bleak and rainy December morning, Francis became the last man hanged in Suffolk County.

1914-- The Dictaphone Murder: Florence Carman

In the summer of 1914, the nation was gripped by the trial of Mrs. Florence Carman, who was accused of killing Mrs. Louise Bailey. But when all was said and done, the victim would never get justice.

On the evening of July 1, 1914, a bullet pierced the window of Dr. Carman's Freeport home office. The shot struck Mrs. Bailey killing her instantly. The reason Mrs. Bailey was at the office may forever be lost to the ages, but it was said she was pregnant, so perhaps she was seeing the doctor for prenatal care? She was in the office after the usual hours. This, of course, led people to suspect that perhaps the doctor was not seeing "Lulu" for professional reasons. The Dr. and his wife claimed they did not know Mrs. Bailey and that she was not a regular patient. This further confused the public.

Mrs. Carman was said to be a very jealous woman, thinking all women were after her husband and she had to stay diligent. It was said she had spied on her husband and another woman a few days before the murder. Whatever she saw made her run into the office and slap both the woman and her husband. Dr. Carman had given the woman money, and Florence insisted on it back. Isn't the patient supposed to pay the doctor? This doctor's wife seems to have had good reason to keep an eye on him.

On the evening of the murder, Mrs. Carman testified that she was in bed, and Dr. Carmen was in his office with Mrs. Bailey. All he saw was a man's arm, gun in hand, poking through the window and next he knew the gun went off, shooting Mrs. Bailey.

Numerous witnesses claimed they saw a "woman in white" on the porch at the time of the murder. George Golde said he did not see the woman in white, but later changed his mind and admitted he did. I guess if everyone

else saw her, he must have, too. Two men said they saw a

man with a straw hat on the street at the time the shots rang

out and many felt it must have been done by one of Dr.

Carman's insane patients. But the police had a focus of

their own.

Mrs. Carman was a notoriously jealous woman and

went to great lengths to find evidence of her husband's

infidelity. She often left the Dictaphone turned on when he

had female patients so she could listen to their

conversations. On one occasion, she slapped and pulled the

hair of a female patient. She was often seen looking

through a window, spying on her husband and his patients,

the very window shattered by the projectile ending the life

of his patient.

The Carman's maid, Celia Coleman, gave Mrs.

Carman an alibi: she was in the house at the time of the

murder. But the police were still suspicious of both Dr. and

Mrs. Carman. After all, here was a woman who was, by all accounts, insanely jealous of all of her husband's female patients. It was said that Florence hid in the attic after the police left on the night of the killing, not the actions of a woman who had nothing to hide. The next morning, she went into the office and took the Dictaphone. Wonder why the police didn't take it?

The police found the window screen braced up and broken glass outside the house.

Those accustomed with modern forensics might questions how glass got on the outside if the assailant broke it from the outside, but not these police. There were rumbles that the police had truly bungled the case. But they did reenact the crime, and a week later arrested Mrs. Carman.

The defense attorney felt confident that Florence Carman would be acquitted; after all, they had an alibi witness, Celia Coleman. Celia, the maid, said that Mrs. Carman was in the house, far from the office, when the shooting occurred. But before the trial, Mrs. Carman's alibi vanished when Celia, who no longer worked for the Carmans, recanted, saying that Mrs. Carman had "crept out the back door" and was not in the house when the murder occurred. The maid said that Mrs. Carman had admitted her guilt. This confession made many people believe that the doctor, not Mrs. Bailey, was the intended target.

During the trial, Mrs. Carman was cool and unemotional, but when the jury informed the judge that they could not reach a decision, she cried. Mrs. Carman was released on $25,000 bail then went out to the country, received guests, resigned her membership in the local suffrage club and challenged the district attorney to try her again. The victim's husband demanded they, "Do anything in our power to convict this woman." The authorities asked for a retrial and got one. This time the jury returned a verdict of not guilty. They just couldn't believe a woman like Mrs. Carman could do something like that.

The last words heard from Florence Carman were, "If I had done it, I would never have gone to the same window." Shut up, Florence, you won!

1907-- Typhoid Mary: The Life of Mary Mallon

In the early 1900s, a woman named Mary Mallon was imprisoned on an island just off shore from Manhattan. She had committed no crime. Most people knew her as Typhoid Mary.

Mary Mallon was born in 1869 in Cookstown, Ireland. Fifteen years later she, like many other Irish women, immigrated to New York, hoping for a better life. She easily found work as a domestic and in 1907, began working as a cook at Charles Henry Warren's rented summer home in Oyster Bay.

In late August, Warren became ill and was diagnosed with typhoid fever, a disease caused by bacteria salmonella typhi and spread by contaminated food and water. Soon Mrs. Warren and two other domestics also became ill. In all, six of the 11 people in the home fell prey to the disease. Symptoms included headache, loss of energy, upset bowels and a high fever. It killed about 10% of those infected.

The owner of this summer house worried that they would never again be able to rent that home after this typhoid outbreak, so he hired an investigator, George Soper, to track down the cause of the disease. From the start, Soper suspected Mary. He checked her employment history and discovered that she had served in seven households, always as a cook. In those houses, 22 people had contracted typhoid and one young girl died.

Soper traced Mary to her current employer and told her that she had been spreading the dreaded disease. He wanted her to give him blood and stool samples. Mary did not take this news very well. Soper said later, "I had my first talk with Mary in the kitchen of this house. . .. I was as diplomatic as possible, but I had to say I suspected her of making people sick and that I wanted specimens of her urine, feces and blood. It did not take Mary long to react to this suggestion. She seized a carving fork and advanced in my direction. I passed rapidly down the long narrow hall, through the tall iron gate, and so to the sidewalk. I felt rather lucky to escape." Mary claimed that she had never been ill and certainly never had typhoid. Soper left but later went to her home where she, again, did not react well, cursing him and sending him on his way.

Soper finally gave up, deciding it was time to bring in the authorities. He handed the case to Hermann Biggs at the New York City Health Department. Biggs sent Dr. S. Josephine Baker to talk to Mary. Mary, however, was no more receptive to Dr. Baker than she had been to Roper. Not willing to take "no" for an answer, the doctor returned with five police officers and an ambulance. The doctor reported that Mary had assaulted her and the police officers and then disappeared. But soon came at them again, yelling that they were persecuting her and she had not done anything wrong. She just wanted to be left alone. She was not sick and did not make anyone else sick. Since she wouldn't give them the samples they needed, they could do nothing else but take her with them. The police put Mary in the ambulance, and the doctor was forced to sit on her all the way to the hospital so she didn't further assault them all.

Mary was taken to Willard Park Hospital where the samples were collected. Typhoid was found in her stool and Mary transferred to North Brother Island where she was quarantined in a cottage. Mary was outraged! She continued to tell anyone who would listen that she was healthy and had been "banished like a leper" with only a dog for company. "This contention that I am a perpetual menace in the spread of typhoid germs is not true. My own doctors say I have no typhoid germs. I am an innocent human being. I have committed no crime and I am treated like an outcast -- a criminal. It is unjust, outrageous, uncivilized. It seems incredible that in a Christian community a defenseless woman can be treated in this manner."

Mary wrote a letter explaining her fate to a local newspaper:

In reply to Dr. Park of the Board of Health I will state that I am not segregated with the typhoid patients. There is nobody on this island that has typhoid. There was never any effort by the Board authority to do anything for me excepting to cast me on the island and keep me a prisoner without being sick nor needing medical treatment....

When I first came here I was so nervous and almost prostrated with grief and trouble. My eyes began to twitch, and the left eyelid became paralyzed .... It remained in that condition for six months. There was an eye specialist [who] visited the island three and four times a week. He was never asked to visit me. I did not even get a cover for my

When in January [1908] they were about to discharge me, when the resident physician came to me and asked me where was I going when I got out of here, naturally I said to N.Y., so there was a stop put to my getting out of here....in April a friend of mine went to Dr. Darlington and asked him when I was to get away. He replied "That woman is all right now, and she is a very expensive woman, but I cannot let her go myself. The Board has to sit. Come around Saturday." When he did, Dr. Darlington told this man "I've nothing more to do with this woman. Go to Dr. Studdiford."

He went to that doctor, and he said "I cannot let that woman go, and all the people that she gave the typhoid to and so many deaths occurred in the families she was with." Dr. Studdiford said to this man "Go and ask Mary Mallon and enveigle her to have an operation performed to have her gallbladder removed. I'll have the best surgeon in town to do the cutting." I said "No....

There is a visiting doctor who came here in October. He did take quite an interest in me. He really thought I liked it here, that I did not care for my freedom. He asked me if I'd take some medicine if he brought it to me. I said I would, so he brought me some Anti Autotox and some pills then. Dr. Wilson had already ordered me brewer's yeast. At first I would not take it, for I'm a little afraid of the people, and I have a good right for when I came to the Department they said they were in my [intestinal] tract. Later another said they were in the muscles of my bowels. And latterly they thought of the gallbladder.

I have been in fact a peep show for everybody. Even the interns had to come to see me and ask about the facts already known to the whole wide world. The tuberculosis men would say "There she is, the kidnapped woman"....

Mary Mallon

No one ever explained to Mary that she might have experienced only a minor case of typhoid and just chalked it up to the flu. This disease then was probably transmitted to her victims through unwashed hands. In September of 1910, a new New York Health Commissioner let Mary out of seclusion, but she had to agree to never cook for others again and to take better "hygienic precautions." Mary tried other kinds of employment such as being a maid and doing other's laundry, but those jobs just didn't pay enough to support her, so she eventually went back to being a cook.

In January of 1915, a typhoid epidemic broke out at the Sloane Maternity Hospital—22 people fell ill and two died. The hospital had recently hired a new cook, Mrs. Brown who was later identified as Mary Mallon. Mary was sent back to North Brother Island where she worked in the hospital's labs. In 1932, Typhoid Mary suffered a stroke and died six years later.

1917: For the Love of a Child: The Death of John de Saulles

Divorce, infidelity and the custody of a 4-year-old boy took center stage in the murder of John De Saulles of Westbury. "I killed him and I am glad I did it" a local constable quoted his ex-wife, Bianca, as saying on August 3, 1917 at the murder scene.

Bianca and John's relationship began in 1911 when John, ex-captain of the Yale football team, met Seniorita Bianca Errazuiz, niece of the former president of Chile. John courted the "fresh from the convent" Bianca in Chile, where her family seemed to have wealth, position and influence. But what they really had was only the appearance of wealth, left over from the days when they were actually wealthy and influential. The relationship started, therefore, on shaky ground, each believing the other was something he or she was not.

Bianca, too, thought that John was wealthy and would support her in the same fashion she enjoyed in Chile. Many believed this was the only reason she married him. She also thought she would have an active social life in New York at the side of her adoring husband. She thought wrong.

Bianca came up with a $10,000 dowry. John ran through half of that in no time. It was said that John "sure was a spender." He sold some of Bianca's stock and pocketed the money. More distressing to Bianca was the fact that John turned cold and inattentive when they arrived back in the United States. John left her at his parents' house in Bethlehem, Pennsylvania, and continued his "single" life at his home in Westbury. The dazzling social life she expected never came to pass, at least not for the two of them together.

He began to work for Woodrow Wilson's presidential campaign. When John visited his wife, he told her that if Wilson won there was an excellent chance John would be appointed Minister of Uruguay, but it would take a lot of money to assure that position. Bianca, lonely and bored and hoping for a better, more exciting life, gave John $37,000. It is not clear how the "poor" Bianca always seemed to come up with the money when her husband needed it.

Wilson won and John got his appointment, but soon after he resigned for reasons unknown. Perhaps John found out there would be actual work involved, which would disrupt his active social life. Or, perhaps he found out that he would actually have to live in Uruguay.

From the beginning, accusations of John's infidelity plagued the marriage and, after the birth of John Jr., the adultery escalated. John took his young son along on some of his liaisons. Bianca recalled John Jr. coming home one day and reporting, "Mamma, Daddy took a lady riding with us." The person, though, most associated with John and his philandering was Joan Sawyer, a popular dance star at the time and who had a dance partner called Rodolfo (later to become Rudolf Valentino). Miss Sawyer was a very successful business woman who owned a nightclub, produced records and published dance instructions

Eventually, Bianca was granted a divorce based on the grounds of John's adultery. It was, however, a messy divorce. During her marriage Bianca had made friends with Rodolfo, the partner of her husband's friend Joan Sawyer. Rodolfo was also friends with a local prostitute, Mrs. Thym. John visited both Joan Sawyer and Mrs. Thym regularly. Rodolfo was prepared to testify to having witnessed John's infidelity. John felt that he could discredit Rodolfo by having him arrested for prostitution. To lessen whatever financial settlement Bianca would receive in the divorce, John intimated that Bianca and Rodolfo had engaged in a sexual relationship. Interestingly, when Rodolfo moved to Hollywood this accusation played a role in him becoming a media heartthrob.

Bianca assumed she would have sole custody of her son, but that was not to be. The settlement provided that John Jr. would spend alternating months with each parent until he started school. Bianca was perplexed. Why, given John's proven infidelity, would he be given even that much visitation? She believed that John and his family's influence and Bianca's limited understanding of the American court system would eventually result in her losing all visitation rights.

John Jr. would come home from his father's house relating stories of the elaborate playground, the pony and puppy he was given, the car rides with his father, and visits to his father's lady friends. Bianca feared that John's powerful friends would help him obtain full custody, a feeling fueled by her son's comments when he returned from his father's Westbury home. "Mother, they tell me I don't belong here . . .," Bianca said her son told her. "They say this isn't my home."

Bianca had hoped that she would be allowed to take her son on a visit to his ailing grandmother in Chile, but the court rejected her request. John had reason to fear that his wife would refuse to return the child to the US and that Chile would not honor his custody arrangement. In addition, with World War I in progress, the safety of the boy could not be assured. So Bianca could either go to see her dying mother alone and leave the child with his father or not see her mother at all.

Bianca's life revolved around her son. She did not spend any time with friends and rarely left the house without the child. She was almost manic in her care for her son, living with the perpetual fear that any hint that she was a neglectful mother would give John cause to take the child away, so leaving him to go see her mother was out of the question.

On the evening of the murder, John had promised to return John Jr. by 9 p.m. although there is some confusion as to the actual arrangement for the boy's visit to his father's home. Bianca believed that the child was only visiting for the day and would be returned that night; John believed this was the beginning of the child's month long stay at his house. Bianca had agreed to the visit which was on a day not a part of the usual rotation because John had told her the child's grandfather and aunt were there.

Before the child was picked up for the visit, Bianca was frantic. When John's servant arrived, Bianca refused her entrance because she had come to the front door instead of the back. Bianca told the woman to leave and have someone with more manners come for the child. A

manservant was then sent for the child and presented

himself at the back door. With no other way to stall for

time, Bianca released the child.

By 9:30 that evening, the child still had not arrived

home, and Bianca phoned John from her house in Roslyn.

His butler said that John Sr. was out for the evening and

that John Jr. was asleep. Bianca decided that she had to

"rescue" her son from John's house. She and a maid drove

to Westbury; Bianca was armed with a pistol concealed by

the fold on her skirt.

When Bianca arrived, she was greeted by John's

sister, Mrs. Rudolph Degener, who took Bianca to John.

John was playing with the child. When Bianca told him that

she wanted to take the child home, John was heard to

respond, "That's no use. You can't have the boy. I want

him. I'm sorry. You and I cannot discuss that. The boy is

mine now." This could certainly be interpreted as his keeping the child permanently, which is certainly how Bianca saw it or as the beginning of the child's monthly visit.

Bianca's worst fears had come true; she was going to lose her son. She drew the pistol and emptied five shots into her ex-husband, in front of her son. Bianca always maintained that she did not go to the house that night to kill her husband. But her former sister-in-law, who witnessed the murder, said that shortly after Bianca pulled the trigger, she declared, "It had to be done...I had to have the child. I had to kill him."

After the shooting, Bianca and her maid sat on the see saw and waited for the sheriff to arrive. The sheriff found a calm and collected Bianca who had remained on the scene, knowing she would be arrested.

Bianca was arrested for the murder of her ex-husband. Her lawyer, Henry Uterhart, told reporters that Bianca felt she had the right to do what she did because of all the pain and suffering she had endured at the hand of John de Saulles. He had promised to return her son and he broke that promise. Bianca's fear that she would lose her son, the one ray of joy in her life, "unhinged her."

The trial was so exciting that it replaced the news of the War on the front page of the newspaper. Her attorney enthralled the jury with the lurid tales of John's infidelities and Bianca's sad tale of a woman whose only concern was the welfare of her young son. The grand jury determined his death a justifiable homicide, and Bianca was a free woman. Bianca and her son moved to San Francisco and then on to Japan. She married and divorced again and lived "in relative obscurity" until her death in 1940.

1931: The Body on the Beach: Who Killed Starr Faithfull?

On June 8, 1931 Starr Faithfull's lifeless body was found on the sandy shore in Long Beach, Long Island. As beautiful in death as she was in life, her long brown hair was draped over an expensive silk dress. She wore nothing else. This was the beginning of a story that ultimately would have no ending.

The medical examiner concluded the cause of death was drowning. Sand found in Starr's lungs indicated she was still alive as she lay in the shallow surf or perhaps she had drowned in the waters of the Atlantic and had washed up on the shore where she had been found. Finger shaped bruises marred her arms, and there was evidence of a sexual assault. An examination of her liver revealed the presence of the sleep-inducing prescription drug, Veronal.

The medical examiner said the cause of death was drowning, but Starr had help.

As the search for her killer began, a disturbing picture of the victim's life emerged. To say that Starr had a traumatic childhood would be an understatement. Starr's father was a ne'er-do-well who never earned enough money to support his family and satisfy his wife, who came from an "impoverished branch of a wealthy family."

Starr attended a local boarding school, her tuition having been paid by contributions from the wealthier side of her mother's family. The principal organizer of Starr's tuition fund was Martha Peters, wife of well-known politician, Andrew Peters. Andrew Peters was the former Mayor of Boston, a congressman, and President Woodrow Wilson's Assistant Secretary of the Treasury. Such a well-connected husband ensured the success of Martha's mission. What prompted this benevolence is not certain.

But, one can speculate that it was a veiled attempt to rescue Starr from the evil clutches of Mr. Peters. When Starr was 11, Peters regularly had her accompany him on trips. They stayed at hotels where he read to her from sex manuals and doused the child with ether to make her less resistant to his sexual advances. In fact, Starr grew to like the effect of the ether, calling it "creamy dreamy." She spent an entire summer with his family in Maine where, with such daily access to Starr, he continued his molestation. Arguably, sending Starr to a boarding school was Mrs. Peters' subtle method of depriving her husband access to Starr in the hope of breaking the pattern of abuse while sparing him (and her) public humiliation.

When Starr was a teen, she began exhibiting odd behaviors, i.e., she was very moody and withdrawn and would dress like a boy to hide her femininity. Perhaps Starr hoped that if she was less physically appealing, her cousin would lose interest in her. It is well documented that these

44

behaviors are exhibited by sexual abuse survivors. Two months before she was due to graduate high school, she dropped out thus launching her slow descent into a life of drugs and alcohol.

During this period, Starr's mother divorced Starr's father and married her neighbor, Stanley Faithfull. She made her daughters give up their father's last name, and from then on they were known as the Faithfull family. With this, Starr's mother erased a whole family's identity. Their new life in Manhattan's Greenwich Village was one of genteel poverty because Stanley had no more financial resources than her previous husband. Still no one in the Faithfull family felt it necessary to find work.

When Starr was 19, she was found dazed, drugged, naked, and beaten in a New York hotel room with a strange man. She was admitted to a mental hospital where she stayed for nine days and was sent on her way to continue her life of self-destruction. This seems an opportunity missed to save this young woman.

In 1924, the family became aware of Andrew Peters' crimes. But, instead of having Peters arrested, the Faithfull family decided to make the most of the opportunity and accepted money to keep this information to themselves. They were paid $20,000, the equivalent of $275, 000 in today's money. This was not the only payment the Faithfull's got from Cousin Andrew. In the end they would have received the equivalent of over a million dollars for the innocence of their daughter.

During the late 1920's, Starr occupied herself with travel, a nine month Mediterranean cruise, seven other ocean voyages, and three long visits to London. One does not have to wonder what Starr wanted to distance herself from. Her mother had taken away her identity and had sold her childhood to the highest bidder. Star had now been betrayed twice by her family: first by Andrew Peters and then by her mother who put money before the pain and suffering of her daughter.

She became a regular on the Manhattan piers where the great liners docked, dropping in on bon voyage parties and disembarking just as the ships prepared to weigh anchor. Was Starr pretending she was still one of those passengers who could retire to their cabins after a night of partying? Imagine her mental state as she walked down the gangplank and waved a sad good-bye to each ship as it steamed away to some exotic destination while Starr made her way back home.

When Starr went missing, her step-father filed a report with the police. Stanley Faithfull presented an image of his step-daughter that made her appear to be a saint and threatened to sue any paper that printed anything to the contrary.

During the search for his missing step-daughter, Stanley asked a police officer, "Do you know how long it will take for a body to come to the surface in a drowning case?" This question confused the officer because there was no indication that Starr was dead let alone having drowned.

But on the morning of June 8, 1931, Mr. Faithfull's hunch became reality when Starr's body was found by a man walking his dog on the beach. She was a sandy mess and not the picture of the beautiful woman seen in the papers the next day. When the coroner declared her death a possible homicide, the newspapers teemed with stories of Starr's sexual exploits. Many of the stories were gleaned from diaries that were found in a search of Starr's room. These diaries documented her sexual adventures and became fuel for the newspapers for days. A common thread running through them was that Starr would often lead men on, only to disappoint them. Remember that incident in the New York hotel room? Her step-father,

48

though, told any and everyone who would listen that there were no diaries that the ones in the paper were not real.

There was speculation about the cause of Starr's death, but her step-father was sure that she had been murdered. One theory he had was that Andrew Peter's had her killed to keep her quiet about the abuse. It was later revealed that just a few days before Starr's death, Stanly went to Peters again for more money. Perhaps Peter thought, "Enough, is enough," and decided to solve his problem permanently. If Starr was gone, there was no one to verify the abuse.

An alternate scenario could include Starr's obsession with George Jameson-Carr, a ship's surgeon. A few days before she died, an intoxicated Starr boarded his ship in search of him. The doctor asked her to leave but Starr stowed away. She was discovered and returned to shore aboard a tugboat. This was not the first time a cruise ship had to resort to such measures to return the stowaway.

When Jameson-Carr returned from sea two weeks after Starr's death, he claimed he had received three letters from Starr in which she revealed a plan to end her "worthless, disorderly bore of an existence." But before she did, she was going to indulge in "a delicious meal with no worry over gaining . . . Also I am going to enjoy my last cigarettes. I won't worry because men flirt with me in the streets - I shall encourage them - I don't care who they are." Could one of these men have killed Starr before she could kill herself?

Starr's stepfather maintained that the letters were forgeries, though the authorities' handwriting experts found the penmanship to be consistent with that in Starr's diaries, Stanly produced his own experts who stated they were indeed forgeries.

Newspapers again speculated about the circumstances of her death. Since she had been seen on the docks and aboard various ships on the day she disappeared, one popular theory was that she had again stowed away and had jumped as the cruise ship passed Long Beach, making her death an accidental drowning.

Still another theory combined both murder and suicide angles: Starr had indeed set out to kill herself, and while enjoying her last meal, met her killer and took him to Long Beach where she could see the lights of the cruise ships. When Starr refused to yield to his advances, the theory went, he killed her, leaving her partially clothed body on the beach.

Throughout the weeks of intense newspaper coverage, Nassau County District Attorney Elvin Edwards maintained his belief that Starr had been murdered. His theory was that she was killed by two men who drugged her and held her head under water. This theory was backed up by the medical examiner. Starr's stepfather accused the D.A. of dragging out the investigation for publicity and told anyone who would listen that this was a political murder. Peters, the relation who had abused Starr for most of her childhood, was said to have suffered a nervous breakdown during this time. Perhaps he feared that more than Starr's sex life and drunken exploits would be revealed during the investigation.

No one has ever been convicted, or even charged, in the death of Starr Faithfull. Who killed Starr Faithfull? Was it the drugs and liquor lifestyle? Or was it Starr herself, who had been abused, misused and abandoned by all she cared about?

1935: Just Your Average Neighbors: Everett Appelgate and Mary Frances Creighton.

The players in this sordid story are a colorful troupe: Ada Appelgate, 36, the victim, weighing in at 224 pounds and said to be rather lazy and very talkative; her husband, Everett Appelgate, 38, who worked as an investigator for the Veterans Unemployment Bureau of Nassau County and fancied himself a lady killer; their friends, John and Mary Frances Creighton, who'd had a little trouble with the law over a poisoned relative or two, and, finally, the Creighton's' 15-year-old daughter, Ruth.

When John Creighton offered to provide shelter for his homeless friends, Everett and Ada Appelgate and their daughter Agnes, the two families found themselves squeezed into the Creighton's Baldwin, Long Island, home. In the home already were Mary Frances and their children, 15-year-old Ruth and 12-year-old Jackie. Ruth and Agnes slept, at first, in a dirty, cramped, cold attic. Neither girl was happy with that situation, so they eventually moved into the room with the Appelgates. Eventually, Ruth would end up in the bed with the couple.

After 10 months, in September, 1935, Ada Appelgate took ill. After a brief hospitalization, she seemed to be getting better and was sent home. A few days later, much to her doctor's shock, Ada died. Her doctor was startled; she just wasn't that sick.

While Ada's body was cooling upstairs, there was a disturbing conversation going on downstairs. Everett, Ruth, Mary and a neighbor discussed Everett's getting married again. Yes, that's right. With Everett's wife's body not even slightly cold yet, there was a chat going on about who should be the next Mrs. Appelgate. The neighbor suggested that a rich old woman might be to his liking, but Everett, looking at Ruth, said, "Funny if I married someone real young." This discussion was at best tacky; at worst it provided Everett with an obvious motive to kill his wife.

But the authorities had no reason to suspect foul play until anonymously mailed newspaper clippings regarding the trial of John and Mary Frances Creighton in the arsenic poisoning death of her brother in Newark, N.J., 12 years before arrived at the Nassau County District Attorney's office. It was alleged that Frances had killed her brother and collected both his life insurance and a small trust fund. She was tried for the crime, and even though there was a great deal of circumstantial evidence, she was acquitted because no one actually saw her purchase the poison or give it to her brother. Later, Mary Frances explained that her brother was ill and in great pain and that she merely "helped" him by ending his life. **After her acquittal,** Mary thought it was clear sailing, but she was immediately arrested for the death of her father-in-law, apparently someone who also needed her "help."

Without a defense even being mounted, the Creightons were again acquitted.

A few days later, Mary Frances Creighton returned to the same courtroom to answer charges that she had poisoned her mother-in-law. Again she was found not guilty. The woman was Teflon® but she realized that it was now time to get out of New Jersey. Three times she had gotten lucky, but she didn't want to push her luck.

But old habits die hard. Ada Applegate's autopsy showed that she died from a dose of arsenic strong enough to kill five men. During their investigation, the police questioned little Ruth Creighton, not believing she would have much to add to their investigation. But, she blurted out - quite to their embarrassed surprise - that she was not a virgin, it was "Uncle" Everett's fault, and her mother knew all about it. Still in shock, the officers let Ruth explain.

Because of the overcrowding in the house, Ruth and the Applegate's' daughter Agnes, 12, had been sleeping in the filthy attic. The two girls finally convinced the Applegate's to let them join them in the warmer bedroom. Eventually, Ruth moved into the Applegate's' bed. Everett stated that this sleeping arrangement contributed to his intimacy with Ruth. Ada must have been a very heavy sleeper to have slept through her husband having sex right next to her. Later, Mary Frances Creighton would also claim an intimate relationship between herself and Everett Appelgate. Mary Frances claimed that Everett used her arsenic-laced past to blackmail her into accepting his sexual relationship with her daughter and with her also sleeping with him and then into poisoning his wife for him. This was a very persuasive man.

Various motives have been proposed for Everett wanting his wife out of the way. Although the most obvious seemed to be to free him to pursue his various sexual relationships. Everett wanted to marry the young girl, but his having a wife stood in the way. Testimony at the trial also suggested that Everett aspired to a high position in the American Legion. But Ada took pleasure in gossiping, even if the gossip was about her own husband. His wife's inappropriate remarks at inopportune times made his goal seem unattainable. How much better it would be to have a young trophy wife to show off while he jockeyed for the high office he sought. How the other Legionnaires would be jealous; they would see he was the kind of man women flocked to. Perhaps, this is why Everett confessed so easily to the affair with the underage girl—he felt it made him seem manly.

Everett and Mary were arrested for Ada's murder. They each testified at their trials. Everett said he knew nothing about poison or poisoning his wife. He pointed out the same thing could not be said for Mary. Mary testified she had nothing to do with it; she had no reason to want

Ada dead, but Everett did. She testified that she had often seen him mix arsenic in Ada's egg nog, bring it to her, and give her a kiss. I guess in Mary's world a little arsenic in the egg nog is nothing to cause alarm.

Everett Appelgate and Mary Frances Creighton were convicted and executed less than a year after Ada Applegate's death. Everett's execution was uneventful as such things go, but Mary Frances was so distraught that she had to be sedated and was unconscious when Ol' Sparky was fired up. **Justice had finally caught up with her.**

1949: Fernandez & Beck: A Love Story?

Hawaiian-Born Raymond Fernandez was a spy during World War II, and after the war, while on a boat, a metal hatch fell on his head, leaving him with extensive brain damage and a large dent in his skull. He also lost his hair and from then on wore a toupee to hide the terrible scar. It is believed that the concussion changed Fernandez's personality from a mild-mannered man to a diabolical seducer and killer of women. After his head injury, Fernandez was arrested for stealing some clothes and was sent to prison. While there, his cellmate got him interested in voodoo and black magic. Fernandez felt it was the black magic that gave him such a hold over women. Raymond eventually moved to Spain where he had a wife and four children. He abandoned them and journeyed to New York where he met up with Martha Beck, a match made in hell.

Martha Beck had been married three times, mostly to men who had gotten her pregnant. To keep from being embarrassed the first time she got pregnant, Martha invented a husband who was in the military. She realized at some point that she would have to produce the fictional husband, so she arranged to receive a telegram stating he had been killed in action. Problem solved.

After working her shifts as a nurse in a military hospital, Martha frequented bars, looking for love and commitment; what she found, however, was only a series of one night stands that eventually resulted in her becoming pregnant for a second time. Upon learning of his impending fatherhood, the putative parent tried to kill himself. This "I'd rather die than be a father to your kid" attitude must have diminished Martha's already flagging self-esteem. Her desperate need to be loved and protected was manifested in a condition best described as sex mad - probably the result of having matured early. Her earliest sexual encounter was at the age of 10 at the hands of her brother.

While working at a funeral home, she met Anthony Beck, who, no surprise, got her pregnant. Anthony and Martha married but after only six months, he deserted her. It is after this final insult that Martha's choice in men goes from bad to worse...she meets Raymond Fernandez.

In 1947, 32-year-old Raymond met Martha Beck, then 27, through a lonely hearts column in the newspaper. Fat, pushy and penniless, Martha wasn't exactly Raymond's type, and, most importantly, she was too poor to con. After their first meeting, Fernandez returned to New York and sent her a "Dear John" letter. This did not deter Beck at all; she arrived on his doorstep, two of her children in tow. Fernandez was impressed at the lengths this woman would go to be with him, so he told her that she could stay, but the kids had to go. Now, for most mothers, this would be a deal

breaker, but not our Martha. Desperate to be with

Fernandez, she swiftly took the children to the Salvation

Army and left them there and never looked back. Not

exactly Mother of the Year material, but one has to ask if

these children were better off without Martha?

So began the "Lonely Hearts Killers." Raymond

would troll the Lonely Hearts columns in the newspaper

then arrive on the doorsteps of these forlorn women with

his "sister" in tow. Myrtle Young of Chicago was one of

their marks. Raymond found her in the newspaper and

started the process to fleece her of her money. The problem

was that his "sister" had to come along on their dates.

When Myrtle grew suspicious of Raymond and his "sister,"

she went to the police to lodge a complaint against them.

As she told her story, Martha stood behind her, winking at

the police officer at the desk. He sent Myrtle on her way

with a suggestion she seek psychiatric care. Raymond and Martha shipped her home with a stomach full of sleeping pills. Myrtle died from a cerebral hemorrhage shortly after returning home. .

Bolstered by the success with their first victim, Raymond again searched the loney hearts column for his next victim. The next of these unfortunate women was Janet Fay of Albany, New York. Fernandez showed up on the doorstep of this lonely-hearts pen pal on New Year's Day, 1949; by January 2, she was on her way to Valley Stream, Long Island, the latest fiancée of Raymond Fernandez.

Martha again posed as Raymond's sister, and within a day was already on Janet Fay's nerves. When Janet complained to Raymond, she received a hammer to her skull from Martha. Having already fleeced the woman of $6,000. Raymond finished her off by strangling her with her own scarf. Janet Fay was buried under a slab of concrete in the basement of their rented house. After the killing, the lovers took in a movie where they gorged themselves on popcorn and soda, celebrating another success.

The deadly duo left Long Island, continuing their spree in Michigan and leaving in their wake the bodies of their final victims, Delphine Downing and her 2-year-old daughter Rainelle. Delphine was a lonely widow who welcomed the attention Raymond lavished on her and her daughter.

In fact, Raymond may have found Delphine and the living situation there to his liking. He offered Martha $2,000 to leave. This was unacceptable to Martha; she had Raymond and was not going to let this woman and her kid spoil everything. Instead, Martha fed Delphine sleeping pills, but not enough to kill her. Raymond's bullet in her head did that. A few days later, when the child wouldn't stop crying for her mother, Martha, at Raymond's request, drowned the child in the basement. It seems that Martha and Raymond had found a taste for killing in addition to hustling these women.

The neighbors, suspicious of the Downing's' disappearance, contacted the police, and Raymond and Martha were arrested. Raymond not only confessed, he bragged, telling police detail after detail about swindling and often killing his numerous victims. He often vacillated between confessing his own guilt and putting all the blame on Martha and her jealousy. While Fernandez confessed, Beck sat next to him, occasionally brushing his hair and adding extra details to the confession. Why it was so easy to get the pair to confess is unclear, excellent police work, perhaps? But once Raymond started, it was his grand performance and he was the center of attention.

Martha, too, appeared rather proud of their exploits, even sending letters to local newspapers with details of their lurid "voodoo sex." But she was upset by the media's descriptions of her as fat and wrote to them complaining.

When the Michigan police found out that New York could execute Raymond and Martha, the two were shipped back to Long Island to be tried for the murder of Janet Fay. The defense was that Beck was insane, citing her numerous suicide attempts. In court, Martha rushed to Raymond's side, lavishing kisses all over his face, leaving him covered in lipstick. Was she hoping this would convince the jury she was crazy or was this just another show of Martha's devotion to Raymond?

After their conviction, Martha and Raymond could see each other from their death-row cells and would often blow kisses to each other. Raymond, whose affections for Martha before their arrest were mostly lukewarm, developed an enormous passion for her at this time, writing in a note to her, "I would like to shout my love for you to the world." Perhaps he had realized that depth of Martha's love for him? Who else ever felt that way about him but Martha?

Before she was executed, Martha wrote in a statement:

"My story is a love story. But only those tortured with love can understand what I mean . . . I am a woman who had a great love and always will have it. Imprisonment in the `Death House' has only strengthened my feeling for Raymond."

On March 8, 1951, Martha Beck and Raymond Fernandez were electrocuted at Sing Sing Prison. It was the custom on days when multiple executions were being held that the person whom the guards felt would deal least well with their impending death would be taken first, and the most stoic person would go last. Martha would be the fourth and last person executed that day. She insisted on having her hair done and looking as good as possible when she sat in the chair. Martha proved too fat to fit in the electric chair and had to sit on the armrest for her execution. Even in the last act of Martha's life, there is humiliation.

1955 `Every Cinderella Has Her Midnight': the Death of the Woodward Family

IN 1943, while the world was at war, Ann Crowell, a 27-year-old aspiring actress, met wealthy 22-year-old William Woodward, Jr. at the Copacabana nightclub in New York City. Thus began a fairy tale relationship destined to have a not so happy ending.

Ann started life as Evangeline Crowell. Proceeds from her father's corn farm in America's heartland were meager leaving the family dirt poor. A teenaged Ann decided she wanted to be more than just a country bumpkin, or to at least appear to belong to a higher class. In pursuit of her dream, Ann moved to Kansas City then traded up to the bright lights and wealth of Manhattan. Ann's good looks enabled her to find employment with the John Robert Powers modeling agency, created by the actor of the same name. Ann was industrious; she subsidized her modeling income with a job as a showgirl at FeFe's Monte Carlo nightclub. It was at FeFe's where she met William Woodward Sr. Soon the rumor mill was abuzz with suggestions that she was the senior Woodward's mistress and when he tired of her, she was passed on to his son. Talk about your hand-me-downs!

William Jr rejected the "proper" life that his parents wanted for him and felt that Ann was the key to his escape. He thought a relationship with Ann would exclude him from the upper crusty society he disliked. But one thing William didn't count on was Ann's desire to embrace that very same society. He soon realized that Ann's desire for the good life would trap him within his despised upper class.

Was it not unexpected that William's family and other members of New York's high society never quite approved of the farm girl turned socialite? William's mother, Elsie Ogdon Cryder Woodward, the reigning queen of the privileged class, opposed her son's plan to marry Ann. On their wedding invitation, Ann wrote that her father was the late Col. J.C. Crowell. In fact, he was now a streetcar conductor named Jesse Claude Crowell who had not seen his daughter in 15 years. He actually thought his daughter was the actress Eve Arden, a natural mistake since she had changed her name to Ann Eden.

In the beginning, Ann and William appeared the model of a loving couple. By all appearances, they were living the good life, shuttling between their Manhattan townhouse and their 45-acre Oyster Bay Cove estate, and racing William's thoroughbred horse Nashua, which won the Belmont Stakes and the Preakness races. Their happiness seemed complete with the births of their two sons, William III and James. But this appearance of happiness hid a dark truth. Both Bill and Ann were playing dueling detectives, trying to determine if one was cheating on the other. Bill met and fell for Princess Marina Tortonia

and asked Ann for a divorce. Ann demanded so enormous

a settlement to end the marriage that Bill eventually

dropped the idea of a divorce and Marina, as well.

To Ann the idea of divorcing Bill was unacceptable.

She didn't want to give up her place on the best dressed

lists and enjoyed chasing down and befriending European

royalty. Photographs of her home appeared in many style

magazines, and her portrait was painted by none other than

Salvatore Dali. But Ann hated the portrait and refused to

pay for it—Dali sued.

But the fairy tale ended abruptly on the night of

October 30, 1955. Ann and William had attended a party

in Locust Valley for their friend, the Duchess of Windsor.

Much of the conversation that night revolved around recent

burglaries in the area. Bill said he had found a shattered

window and that his bathhouse and cabana had been broken

into. William told a guest that he and Ann were so concerned for their safety that each slept with a gun. But even with the talk of the robberies, people said they were in good spirits and left the party around 1 a.m.

After returning from the party, Ann and William retired to their respective bedrooms. A couple of hours later, both were awakened by a noise in the house. Ann, armed with her 12-gauge shotgun, stepped into the hall separating her bedroom from her husband's. She observed a shadowy figure in the murky darkness. Believing it to be the burglar, she fired her weapon, mortally wounding not a burglar but her husband, William.

Ann called the police, but not before calling her lawyer. When the police arrived, Ann said, "Almost immediately, I realized it was my husband. I ran to him and fell on the floor beside him." Ann's attorney arrived and arranged for her to be taken to Doctor's Hospital, where her attorney said she was too distraught to speak any further to the police

William's funeral was held while Ann was recovering in the hospital. She eventually told her story to the police.

Within a day or two, William's family hired private detectives to see if there would be reason to doubt Ann's story. There was evidence that all had not been well in the marriage. Ann had previously hired her own private investigators to see if William was cheating on her. "I just wanted to satisfy my curiosity," she told them. They never found any evidence of infidelity.

Some friends spoke of the Woodward's ideal marriage; others revealed their frequent public quarrels and Ann's displays of jealousy, such as the time she ripped the pearls off a woman she suspected of having an affair with William.

Less than a month after William's death, a grand jury cleared Ann after her 25-minute testimony. Her case was helped in part by the testimony of Paul Wirths, a 22-year-old German immigrant who was a suspect in the local burglaries. He admitted to police that he was in the general area at the time of the shooting. Police said he had broken into the Woodward's' garage a few days before and slept in their car.

Ann's mother-in-law stood behind Ann in public, mostly because she felt that having their mother in prison would scar her grandsons for life. Ann received millions from Bill's death, but it was not given to Ann directly. It was in trust with her mother-in-law as the trustee. Funds were doled out to Ann as needed, just enough to keep her living the good life, but not enough for her to be free of Elsie. After the inquest, Ann sent her sons to boarding school and spent most of her time in Europe, trying to come to terms with the death of her husband. Ann found that many of society's doors that had been open to her were now closed.

In the years after the accident, Ann and William's sons led very different lives. Jimmy, against the family's wishes, fought in Viet Nam. His life devolved into a world of alcohol and drugs. He befriended Xavier Holland of *Happy Hooker* fame, who wrote a chapter in her book titled "Jimmy, Don't Jump Again." In 1976, he took his life by jumping from a hotel window.

His brother, William III, went to Harvard, was a journalist in the late 60s, ran for public office, and was New York State Deputy Superintendent of Banks. He was said to have the manner of a European prince. William married and had one daughter. After his marriage failed, some say he became despondent at not seeing his daughter as often as he wanted. At age 54, he, too, jumped to his death from the window of his apartment.

Ann Woodward's story was grist for at least two works of fiction: Dominick Dunne's "The Two Mrs. Grenvilles" and Truman Capote's "Answered Prayers". Prior to publication of the Capote article, friends say Ann was shown an advance copy. The character representing her was portrayed as guilty of her husband's murder. It was suggested that the 1975 release of the first few chapters of Capote's book in Esquire magazine prompted Ann Woodward's suicide in her Park Avenue home. Her mother-in-law remarked, "She shot my son, and Truman just murdered her, and so now I suppose we don't have to worry about that anymore."

The director of a film later made from Dominick Dunne's book said he kept a quote from the Claudette Colbert film "Midnight" in front of him to help explain the main character.

"Every Cinderella," it said, "has her midnight."

1956: Peter Weinberger: A Community Wakes Up

In the 1950s on Long Island, many babies' afternoon naps were spent in carriages parked in front of their homes; that is until July 4, 1956 when young Peter Weinberger was taken from his carriage. And was never seen alive again. From that day on, children on Long Island took their nap indoors.

That fateful day, Peter's father, Morrie, took the Weinberger's 2 ½ year old son to the post office while his wife, Beatrice, put 33 days old Peter down for his nap around three p.m. Before placing Peter in his carriage, Beatrice dressed him in his white and yellow kimono and hat.

Ten minutes later, Beatrice noticed that the netting she had placed over the carriage was moved. Pinned to the tiny pillow was the following note: "Attention: I'm sorry this had to happen, but I am in bad need of money, and couldn't get it any other way . . . Just put $2,000 00/100 (Two thou- sand) in small bills in a brown envelope, and place it next to the sign Post at the corner of Albermarle Rd. and Park Ave at Exactly 10 o'clock tomorrow . . .."

The police were summoned. The first officer at the scene called his superior and related what he believed had happened, but the dispatcher was confused at first. Nothing like this had happened before on Long Island.

The Weinbergers raised the ransom from family and friends, and the bank agreed to open, even though it was a holiday. The press was asked to keep the story out of circulation in case it scared off the kidnappers. But *The Daily News* didn't follow the police's request. The newspaper claimed they never got the message. After that, the papers had a "free for all" with the story.

With the story out, the police decided to use it to their advantage by holding a news conference where it was reported that the baby needed a medically recommended formula available only from a pharmacy. Pharmacists where advised to let the police know of anyone requesting this "special" formula. This was not true, but the police hoped-it would lead them to the kidnapper

On the day of the ransom drop, the police realized that the instructions were confusing because there were two places where Albermarle crosses Park, so they left an envelope at each intersection. But, due to all the publicity, crowds had gathered in front of the Weinberger's house and in the neighborhood, which probably frightened the kidnappers who never appeared at either site

After a second ransom drop also went uncollected, Mrs. Weinberger got the following call:

"Hello, Mrs. Weinberger?"

"Yes."

"Listen, do you want to see your kid or don't you?"

"Er, who is this?"

"Well, it's the party you would be interested in. I called up earlier. And I don't know who answered. I made an appointment and nobody showed up."

"You made an appointment with my husband? What did you ask him to do?"

"Go over to Exit 26 and -"

"Yes, we kept that appointment. My husband went."

"Nobody was there. I was there for over an hour. Well, now, on Exit 28, if you want, right by the sign, I'll be there in at most a half hour. You'll find a blue bag there."

"Now, wait a minute. Let me get this straight. I'm nervous. Just what do you want me to do?"

"Put the money in and take the note and it'll tell you where you'll find the baby in an hour's time."

"Wait a minute. Where on Exit 28, which side?"

"As you're going towards New York. And you will find a blue bag right by the sign - not at the exit, right by the sign that says, `Exit 28.' "

"You're only giving me a half hour?"

"That's all. You can make it in fifteen minutes. I know. I already done it. I'll be watching as you go by."

"The blue bag will be right by the sign that says `Exit 28'?"

"That's right."

The Weinbergers received numerous similar crank calls demanding the ransom. Mr. Weinberger always complied, but no one ever picked up the money

The note itself was the best lead to the kidnapper, so the police proceeded to take writing samples from all who had any kind of contact with the child or the Weinberger family, friends, Weinberger's employees, deliverymen, paper boys, meter readers, diaper service drivers, and milk men

A man by the name of Angelo LaMarca was a match for the writing and was taken to the FBI's Manhattan headquarters, where the local police were excluded from the questioning. The agents finally got a confession from LaMarca, but his story never really stayed consistent. In one version, he had an accomplice and in another he was alone. He never admitted the child was dead, yet led the authorities to a weedy area on the side of the Northern State Parkway's service road. They found Peter's tiny skeleton, diaper and the yellow blanket. LaMarca had panicked and tossed the baby there where it died from exposure and starvation

LaMarca was a 31-year-old drop-out who had failed at everything he attempted to take care of his family. He and his wife had purchased a home in Plainview, but from the start had trouble paying the mortgage. They owed money to everyone they knew. La Marca thought the kidnapping was the only way he could raise the cash to catch up on his mortgage and pay his debts. He claimed the kidnapping had not been planned. As he drove around aimlessly, he took the child simply because Peter had been left outside unattended.

LaMarca pled not guilty by reason of insanity, but the jury found him guilty and sentenced him to death, feeling he could have returned and saved the child when the drop off failed. He was executed at Sing Sing prison on August 7th, 1958.

This became a cautionary tale to all mothers who had previously left their babies outside for their naps. Long Island had become just a little less safe.

1974: The Real Amityville Horror: Ronald DeFeo

The story of Ronald DeFeo Jr. is related here in three parts. First, there is the tale of a greedy son whose avarice led him to slaughter his family to collect an inheritance. The second is the fairytale of 112 Ocean Avenue, the infamous house where the DeFeo murders took place and put Amityville on the paranormal map. And the final story includes all the subsequent and numerous stories young Mr. DeFeo has told since his incarceration to stretch out his 15 minutes of fame.

In the front yard of 112 Ocean Avenue, Amityville, a religious shrine to St. Joseph used to greet visitors to the DeFeo home. Neighbors described the family as "close-knit" and the DeFeos as devoted parents. There was little evidence that their children didn't deserve that devotion –

except, perhaps for Ronald Jr., the black sheep of the family.

Ronald Jr. was a wild, undisciplined troublemaker who was either thrown out or dropped out of every school he attended. The pattern persisted after he graduated with accusations of theft and absenteeism following Ronald from job to job. He did his best to crack the perfect façade his parents wanted to present to the world.

Our story begins in the pre-dawn hours on November 13, 1974. Evidence at trial exposed that Ron Jr. snuck into his parent's bedroom and first shot his father; Ronald's mother was awakened by the shots that killed her husband. Moments later she, too, was shot to death as she struggled to get out of bed to reach one of the many guns usually kept in the room. When DeFeo Jr. was finished, the dead included his mother and father; his sisters Dawn, 18, and Allison, 13, and his brothers Mark, 11, and John, 9.

During questioning by police, Ronald said he had arrived home at about 6 a.m. and found the front door locked. Crawling in through an open window, he found his parents dead in their beds. He then went to a local bar to enlist aid from the patrons, who came back to the DeFeo house and called police.

When Ron Jr was taken to police headquarters, interrogated and put in a cell, he promptly fell asleep. In that first interview, he had insisted he had no knowledge of guns, but while he slept, his friends contradicted that. Also, in his interrogation, he said he thought that Louis Falini, who he said was in the Mafia, had killed his father. At one point, Ron claimed that he was forced to watch Falini commit the murder.

If the interrogation had lasted any longer, he probably would have blamed the dog. But, ultimately, Ronald confessed to all the murders: "Once it started, I just couldn't stop. It went so fast." Ronald later asserted that the

police had beaten that confession out of him. And at trial,

under direct examination, Ronald said he killed them all in

"self-defense." If you didn't write it all down, you couldn't

keep track of which story Ron Jr. was using on any given

day. But it would eventually get even more complicated

once Ron was in prison.

After all the evidence was presented at trial, Ronald

DeFeo Jr. was sentenced to 150 years to life in prison.

Ronald DeFeo Jr.is currently incarcerated at Green Haven

Correctional Facility in Stormville, N.Y.

Usually once the murderer is found, convicted, and

sent to prison, the story is over, but not this one. In

December 1975, George and Kathy Lutz bought the

DeFeo's house for $80,000, way below the market value

for such a house but luckily within the Lutz's price range.

This house, at that price, was very enticing; it had a

swimming pool and boat house with six bedrooms located on a canal. For an extra $400, some of the DeFeo's furniture was included.

Now you may wonder what kind of people buy a house with such a horrific background. Perhaps someone who can spot a bargain, or perhaps for other reasons that might become clear as we go on.

On moving in, George asked a priest come to bless the house, not an odd thing to do since he was aware of what had happened in that house only 13 months earlier. The priest declared that there was a room that was ice cold (maybe faulty pipes?) and a voice told him to "Get out!". His hands began to turn blue, and a few days after he left the house, he suffered flu-like symptoms. Now for many of us that might have been a deal breaker, but the Lutzes claim he never told them what had happened.

Immediately, the Lutz family claimed that the house was haunted and that for the 28 days they lived there, they were tormented by glowing red eyes staring at them from their window, the front door being blown off the hinges, demonic and cold spots in the house where George could never get warm even though he ran the fireplace night and day. Every night, George woke up at 3:15, the time of the DeFeo murders. The young daughter claimed that her imaginary friend, Jodie, often appeared to her as a large pig with glowing red eyes. The children began sleeping on their stomachs, exactly the way the DeFeo children had been found dead in their beds and contrary to the way they had slept before moving in the DeFeo house. Kathy began to have graphic dreams of the murders. In addition, even though it was the dead of winter, the house was constantly full of black flies and a hoof print was seen in the snow outside the house. Weird smells permeated the house that no amount of spray could combat.

George claims to have found a hidden room that did not appear in any of the blueprints for the house. The room was painted red and was a mere four feet by five feet. The Lutze's dog did not like this room and growled anytime the door to it was opened.

George was especially affected. He began to believe he bore a resemblance to Ron Jr. and began to drink at the same bar that Ron Jr. had. He would hear a marching band tuning up and when he went to investigate, he found nothing. In fact, every phenomenon he heard, he was unable to find. This coupled with red welts on Kathy, locked doors being blown off their hinges, slime oozing from the walls, and revolving crucifixes, caused the family to rethink how much they loved this house.

On the night of January 13th, 1976, the family fled the house in terror after the children's beds slammed up and down on the floor, and George was pinned to his bed with his wife levitating above it. They spent the night at Kathy's mother's house and, subsequently, left the state and moved to California. It is unclear how they were able to afford the move; however, in 1977, a book on their experiences called *The Amityville Horror: A True Story* by Jay Anson was published. It was an immediate hit and spawned movies and other media. Perhaps that was how they afforded it.

This was the official story that has been told in books and movies, but DeFeo's attorney, William Weber, Esq., claims that he and the Lutzes gathered one night, consumed copious bottles of wine and concocted a story of a haunted house. Somehow this story was going to help Ron Jr. get out of jail?

Eventually, these claims would be debunked. The hinges on the door supposedly ripped from its hinges was in fact intact. The Lutz family claimed to have called the police numerous time, but no calls were received. The Catholic Church insisted they never sent a priest to the house. The demonic hoof print could not have been seen in the snow since it had not snowed at any time the Lutzes were there. And we could go on, but you get the idea. These things just did not happen, but they make a great story, right?

The house sold again for $55,000 but the family lived there for only two years. They said the reason they left was that they were constantly being bothered by tourists and ghost hunters, which intensified after the film version of *The Amityville Horror* was released, not because of any paranormal activity. Both the new owners and DeFeo's attorney sued the Lutzes and finally got George to admit it was all a hoax concocted to make money. This has to go down as the most lucrative hoax of all time.

The Story 10 Years Later

Years in prison gave Ronald time to come up with other stories of what happened. First was that Dawn actually killed the family because her father wouldn't let her go to Florida with her boyfriend. Ronald said when he heard the shots, he ran upstairs, fought with his sister, threw her against a wall, and then shot her in the back of the head. Another of his stories was that a lady dressed in black had told him to kill his parents.

Ten years later, in an interview in Attica, Ronald told a new story. First, he claimed that he was married a month before the killings and had an 11-year-old daughter. Geraldine, Ronald Jr.'s wife, sat beside him during the telling of this new story. Ronald Jr. said that prior to the murders he was dating Geraldine who became pregnant. His father forced him to marry her. He was telling this new story because his daughter was being harassed and called the anti-Christ, by whom we are not sure. There are no official records of either the marriage or the birth of a child. Even William Weber, DeFeo's attorney, was not aware of the marriage or the existence of a child. The district attorney said that this was just another attempt by DeFeo to bring himself back into the limelight. Prison can get boring.

The skinny drug addict who entered Attica a decade before had transformed himself into a muscular, calm soft-spoken man who, during the interview, claimed that the murders centered on his mother and his sister, Dawn, with his mother having killed Dawn, the three other children and then herself. He is not clear what reason Mrs. DeFeo would have to kill her children, her husband, perhaps, but the children, no.

He had kept quiet up until now because he feared his grandfather, Michael Brigante Sir and his uncle, Peter DeFeo, would harm Ronald's family. His mother, Louise, was extremely close to her father; he showered her with gifts, paid the mortgage, and employed both her husband and her son. Any story that made her the killer would greatly upset him. But, now Michael and Peter were dead, so Ronald felt he had nothing to fear.

In this new version, Ronald Sr. was portrayed as a loud man who dominated his family and beat his wife and children. He worked for his wife's father, the previously mentioned Brigante, but sold stolen motor boat engines on the side, an activity that Ronald Jr. also participated in. Ronald Jr. said that he turned to drugs to escape his father's abuse and overbearing control over his families' lives.

. On the night of the killings, November 12, 1974, Ronald Jr., his new bride and her brother were hanging out, drinking and doing heroin, something they did regularly. With them were her children from another relationship. At 8 p.m. Ron's mother called to tell him that Dawn and her father were fighting, and she needed him to come home. Ron Sr.'s wife was already talking about divorce, so this new betrayal by Dawn had put him over the edge.

Ron Jr. and his brother-in-law arrived at the DeFeo house to cool things down. Ron Jr. had Dawn leave the house for a while and all seemed to calm down. Ronald and his brother-in-law went to the basement and stayed a while playing pool. With everything seemingly calmed down, they were about to leave when they heard a gunshot. They found a rifle on the floor in the hall and his mother and father in their bed. Dad was dead and mother wounded. Outraged (at what, we are not sure), Ron Jr. shot his mother. That's the new story. Yes, there are holes you could drive a truck through and many, many unanswered questions. But logic has never been this killer's strong suit.

The Story 32 Years Later

Thirty-two years after the murders, Ronald gave another interview and another story about what happened that night. Ron had become thin, balding, and extremely agitated. It seemed that he wanted to make sure people could see that it was impossible for one person to have committed the murders of six people with all of them still asleep in their beds.

He again elaborated on the abuse he suffered at the hands of his father, claiming that at one point his father had knocked out a few of his teeth. This abuse was what fueled Ron Jr.'s heroin addiction. Even one of his friends from the time of the killings admitted that it was a "crazy house, with someone yelling all the time."

Ron Jr. stated that in November of 1974, Ron Sr. broke a pool cue over Junior's head and that apparently was the last straw. Ron Jr. decided his father had to die. On the night of the murders, Ron claimed his sister Dawn had been angry at her father and wanted to kill him. Ron went and got a gun and encouraged her to do it. But she was hesitant. Wanting only to scare his father, Ron yelled out, "Hey, Fatman," which woke his father. Ron was startled and shot him. Seeing his mother reaching for her gun on the night stand, Ron shot her. He then went for a drive to clear his head and decide what he was going to do. When Ron returned, he discovered that Dawn had killed the children.

According to Ron, Dawn had always hated her little sister.
Ron and Dawn struggled for the gun and during the
commotion he shot Dawn. This is his last story (well, as of
2017).

The Amityville Horror is known to the world as a
house in Amityville possessed by evil spirits, but if
anything or anyone possessed that house it is the spirits of
the family who lost their lives there at the hands of the real
Amityville Horror—Ronald DeFeo.

1984 "Say You Love Satan": Ricky Kasso

On June 16, 1984, Ricky Kasso, Jimmy Troino and Albert Quinones killed Gary Lauwers. Was it a drug deal gone bad or, perhaps, part of a satanic ritual?

Ricky Kasso, the son of a football coach, grew up in Northport. He did not have an easy life. As a teen he often ran away. He called the streets his home, sometimes living in cars and occasionally a friend's house. Ricky experimented with an assortment of pharmaceuticals such as marijuana, LSD, PCP, and mescaline. His favorite was acid; hence, he was often called The Acid King. He became hooked and began selling drugs to support his habit.

He favored listening to AC/DC, Judas Priest, and Ozzy Osbourne and his reading preferences were books such as Anton LaVey's book, *The Satanic Bible*.

Ever the Renaissance rebel Ricky also got involved in the occult and Satanism, going so far as to join the

"Knights of the Black Circle," a loosely organized group from Northport High school. His membership carried with it the privilege of assisting with satanic rituals, including Walpurgisnacht, a ceremony for the arrival of spring, which was allegedly performed at the infamous DeFeo home in Amityville.

Ricky also was arrested for grave robbing, taking parts of the skeleton, particularly the skull. While in jail, Ricky came down with pneumonia. His being in the hospital prompted his parents to beg the doctors to admit him. After completing their psychiatric observations, the doctors concluded that Ricky was antisocial. This condition did not warrant his being admitted for treatment. Ricky was free to resume his defiant behavior.

Into Rick's life came Gary Lauwers, a fellow drug dealer. One day while Ricky was passed out, Gary, ever the opportunist, took advantage of the situation and absconded with 10 bags of Ricky's angel dust. When confronted,

Gary returned half and promised to pay for the remaining half. But Gary didn't pay up, even after repeated beatings.

Apparently Ricky decided to take the "high" road, telling Gary that he wanted to bury the hatchet. They decided on a time and place to meet. When Gary arrived, present were Ricky and his friends Jimmy and Albert. After sharing mescaline, they started a small fire with kindling found in the woods. Ricky suggested they use some of Gary's hair. Then begins the carnage.

High on PCP, Ricky bit Gary's neck. Gary's socks and jacket were tossed into the fire, and Ricky wrestled with Gary, biting him on the neck and stabbing him in the chest while Albert held Gary down. At one point during the fray, Gary tried to run, but Albert caught him and dragged him back. The assault lasted for hours. Gary's eyes were gouged out, and he was stabbed 35 times. Ricky commanded Gary to say "I love Satan," but instead Gary said "I love my mother." This was the last thing he would say. Before leaving Gary in the woods, Ricky filled Gary's mouth with stones.

During the days after the murder, Ricky took friends to see the corpse, bragging that black crows had delivered a message from Satan requiring a human sacrifice – specifically Gary.

On July 1st, 1984, the police learned that the teens were talking about a body in the woods, and on the 4th of July, cadaver dogs located Gary's body which was little more than a pile of bones cleaned by worms. Since all the teens had said that they had been taken to see the body by Ricky, the police arrested Ricky who was wearing an AC/DC tee shirt at the time and locked him behind bars.

Three days later, Ricky hung himself in his cell. Did the Devil make him do it?

1985: Cheryl Pierson: Daddy's Little Girl

In September 1985, a homeroom discussion regarding a woman who had hired someone to kill her husband inspired the plot to murder Cheryl Pierson's father. Two months later Sean Pica, Cheryl's classmate, stood outside Pierson's house prepared to shoot James Pierson Sr. when he stepped into the early morning cold.

James Pierson Sr. was a "gruff, loud-mouthed, aggressive, generous and loyal" union electrician who always put his family first and worked hard to give them everything they wanted and needed. As a father, he was strict, a man who taught his children to be silent around adults, help with the housework, and always say "please" and" thank you." He could also be indulgent; he would threaten to beat the children if they disobeyed, but never did, and when they obeyed, he showered them with gifts.

In 1979, Cheryl's mother, Kathleen, was diagnosed with a rare form of kidney disease. The family endured numerous trips to doctors and dialysis appointments. Eventually, Kathleen would undergo two kidney transplants. For six years, she was the focus of the family. Cheryl became a surrogate wife and mother. She did all the housework and tended to her sister, JoAnn, and brother, James Jr. which made her feel loved and appreciated.

Sean Pica was not the sort of kid one would expect to get in trouble - a Boy Scout with braces on his teeth and peach fuzz on his face. On that September morning when the homeroom was abuzz with the news about a local woman who had hired a hitman to kill her husband, the comment was made, "Who would do a crazy thing like that?" Sean responded he would for $1,000. Cheryl, overhearing this, said, "I want someone killed." So Cheryl and her boyfriend, Robert, hired Sean, paying a $400 deposit and the balance upon completion of the contract.

Shortly after 6 a.m. on that infamous day, James Sr. dressed and woke up his sleeping children, including Cheryl who had missed school the day before because she over slept. A cup of hot coffee in hand, he stepped out his back door, and Sean Pica, lying in wait, shot him five times, once from behind a tree and four more times at close range.

The police thought it was a professional hit, and were looking in that direction until a classmate of Cheryl's told them about the request for a hitman.

On February 13, 1986, Sean and Cheryl were arrested for plotting to kill her father. Cheryl's boyfriend was charged with conspiracy for providing the first installment payment to Pica.

Cheryl's defense was that she only did this after years of sexual abuse at the hands of her father. During her mother's long illness, Cheryl said she and her father would watch television in his room, soon they shared the bed together, and he began touching and molesting her. "I'd put a pillow over my face. I'd block it out until it was over." She said he continued touching her inappropriately while they drove to the hospital to visit her dying mother. Cheryl would often lash out at her father, "I don't believe you. You've got a wife in the hospital. She's in a coma and you're touching me."

Her father told her that he touched her out of love, but that she should never tell anyone. "The closer we got, the more possessive he got...I did what he wanted to avoid tension in the house." If Cheryl did not comply willingly, other members of the family would feel James Sr.'s wrath. Even Cheryl's mother thought Cheryl and her father were getting too close, but she was too ill to do anything about it.

When Cheryl started dating Robert Cuccio, her father's sexual demands increased; he was obviously jealous and wanted to make sure Cheryl would still be there for him. Cheryl considered suicide as a way to end the abuse, but she worried about her younger sister JoAnn. JoAnn had started to watch television with their Dad.

The story that Cheryl was telling did not sit well with her grandmother and aunt: "Nobody can tell me that my son did this to his daughter." Even her little sister JoAnn, who Cheryl claims to have been protecting, thought her sister was lying. This might have been why Cheryl claimed that she didn't tell anyone about the abuse because she thought no one would believe her.

Both Cheryl and Sean pled guilty to manslaughter. The penalty for Cheryl was up for debate. One way of thinking was that if she was given a long sentence it would send the wrong message to sexual abuse victims, while others felt that no jail at all would cause a "rash of excusable murders." Sean Pica was given 8-24 years while Cheryl got three months.

While they were in jail, Cheryl wrote to Sean, "I had to get a lot of things off my chest. I felt bad that his family got involved in this mess... I wrote to let him know I was still his friend." He wrote back "Hang in there."

When Cheryl was released, she was picked up in a white limousine by her boyfriend, Robert, who had received probation for his part in the murder. She waved from the roof of the limo and was whisked off to the Coram Diner for breakfast where the waitresses picked up the tab: "She's been through enough."

At Robert's home, Cheryl found yellow ribbons around the trees and a turkey dinner waiting. She opened presents, and later that day, she and Robert got engaged. Cheryl and Robert married and have two daughters. She did not reunite with her family.

As for Sean, he spent 16 years in Sing Sing prison where his first years did not go well - numbing himself with drugs and twice being placed in solitary confinement. While in confinement, Sean decided he needed to turn his life around. To that end, he earned not only his high school diploma, but his Bachelor and Master's degrees. He mentored other prisoners, both while in prison and after. When he was released in 2010, he went to work at the East Harlem housing project. Sean is the Executive Director of Hudson Link for Higher Education, which provides college education, life skills and re-entry support to incarcerated and formerly incarcerated.

1987-- Christmas Eve Nightmare: Death of Lisa Solomon

On Christmas Eve 1987, Lisa Solomon's dream of a fairytale marriage came to a tragic end at the hands of her own Price Charming, Matthew Solomon.

Lisa Weaver and Matthew Solomon met shortly after Lisa's graduation from high school. Matthew worked at a gas station near Lisa's home and would whistle at her as she walked past. Lisa's mother said there was an instant attraction. But the relationship was rocky from the start, filled with arguments mostly because of the possessive nature of Matthew. After they were engaged, this did not end and the engagement was off and on for quite a while before they finally married.

Matthew and Lisa married on October 25, 1987. It was a small wedding followed by a reception in Huntington. This was the happiest day of Lisa's life, and she danced every dance with her new husband. No one could expect that in just two months, Lisa's life would be snuffed out at the hands of her groom.

Christmas Eve started out as the intimate, private celebration the newlyweds planned. It was a special night. Not only was it Christmas Eve, but it was the second anniversary of their engagement. They made a pact that night that it would be a tradition - every Christmas Eve they'd go back to Tee-T's where Matthew had proposed. They did the first year, but for their first Christmas as man and wife, Lisa wanted to spend the night in their new home, just the two of them.

Matthew brought home the lobsters for dinner and two bottles of champagne. The young couple shopped for the rest of their seafood dinner together. Matthew, the chef for that night's dinner, sent Lisa to their bedroom when he was cooking the live lobsters since Lisa loved lobster, but didn't like seeing them put into the pot.

After dinner, the two settled down to watch a soap opera that Lisa always taped. While he may have wanted to stay awake, the champagne and having gotten up at 4 a.m. caught up with Matthew and he fell asleep. Lisa woke him, angry he had fallen asleep on Christmas Eve, their special night. Matthew claimed that he told her, that it was "just a soap opera", and she apologized and said she was just depressed. After they talked about Lisa's mother and her father's failing health, Matthew claimed that Lisa wanted to go out for a drive, but Matthew wouldn't let her because he didn't think she should be driving after consuming so much champagne. He claimed she then went out for a walk.

That is the story as Matthew Solomon told it to the police and Lisa's parents early Christmas morning. The search was one of the largest and most intense Long Island had ever seem. Helicopters and search dogs combed Huntington with the help of a psychic and 50 members of the Cross Island Motorcycle Club, the Suffolk Chapter of the Harley Club and the Blue Knights, a police motorcycle club. Matthew was said to be numb and unable to stop crying. The police, at first, didn't suspect foul play because they were told that Lisa had done this kind of thing before.

The grief-stricken newlywed held a press conference on the lawn of his home. His grief and anger showed when he told the press he knew his wife was alive and the person who had taken her should hope the police get to him first before Matthew did. (Personal note: this is the point where I turned to my husband and said, "he killed his wife).

Two men, one of them Lisa's cousin, Steven Klerk, and Karl Heidenreich, searched with a large group on that bitter cold January night. Klerk hoped Lisa was sitting bewildered in some bus station or railroad station or some diner somewhere,

The two men broke off from the large group and decided to search Huntington Station. Looking at the map, the two decided that a farm a little more than a mile from the newlywed's home seemed desolate enough to hide the girl and decided to look there before calling it a night.

Klerk found three garbage bags; two contained leaves but the third contained the frozen body of Lisa Solomon. The family was devastated; they truly expected to find Lisa safe and sound…everyone except Matthew who had known all along that they would not find her safe nor sound.

The search for Lisa ended and now the search for Lisa's killer began. They didn't really search that far.

Matthew was the first and only suspect from the moment the body was found. It was not because Matthew had done or said anything suspicious. Assistant District Attorney Edward C. Jablonski, chief of the Suffolk District Attorney's Homicide Bureau claimed; it was logical since he was the last to see her alive and was also her closest relative.

For 11 days, the police methodically pieced together a case against Matthew, collecting hair and blood samples from him and physical evidence from Lisa's body. They searched both of their cars and the couple's apartment. The apartment was identified as the crime scene and the car as the mode of transportation for the body.

The police saw this as kind of a Leopold and Loeb thing where the suspects were as helpful as possible to the police. Matthew willingly gave up his fingerprints, hair and blood samples. He opened his life up to the police, letting them search anywhere they asked. This level of cooperation was supposed to make him a less likely suspect, but all it did was make the detectives lean more in his direction and make their job easier.

When the evidence contradicted Matthew's story, he was placed under arrest for the murder of his wife. Shortly after the arrest, Matthew, when presented with the evidence from his car, was convinced to confess. He told them that around midnight Lisa, upset, woke him up. She was mad he had fallen asleep on their special night. She told him she was going out. Not wanting her to leave, Matthew said he grabbed her hand and held her, but she bit his arm. He them put his right arm around her neck and squeezed. A minute later, Lisa stopped struggling.

Almost a year later, Matthew stood trial for the murder of his wife. Emotions ran high for Matthew as he was forced to not only face what he had done to his wife but also to his family. He sat for most of the trial with his head in his hands weeping when the court played his conversation with his father when he told him he was the one who had killed Lisa. His father vowed to stand by him no matter what.

Both sides agreed that Matthew had caused the death of his wife, but the prosecution said it was intentional and the defense claimed it was accidental. The jury decided it was second degree murder, and Matthew was sentenced to 25 years to life.

When the verdict was read, there was more high emotion from both sides. Matthew's family was angry at Lisa's, His father, Jack, stood and screamed at Diane Weaver, Lisa's mother, "You got your pound of flesh!" Court officers surrounded him. Later, he stormed from the courtroom yelling, "The lies you've been telling will come out!"

Lisa's family was equally verbal about the verdict; Mrs. Weaver broke into tears. This family had not won anything with this verdict. They had still lost Lisa and the bright future she had seen with Matthew. There would be no little ones, grandchildren to cuddle and adore.

1989: Richard Angelo: The Angel of Death

Richard Angelo had a hero complex. He wanted to be the guy who showed up just in the nick of time to save the day. Richard joined the volunteer fire department to demonstrate his heroism, but that was not enough. He was just one of many who heeded the call to save lives and property. But there were no damsels in distress he could run in to save, nor desperate mothers tossing babies from windows into his outstretched arms. So, Richard moved on.

At age 26, Richard was hired as a nurse at Good Samaritan Hospital. He chose to work the 11:00 p.m. to 7:00 a.m. shift caring for cardiac patients. He chose this shift because of the lack of doctors and the absence of visitors' prying eyes. This would be the perfect setting for his heroics.

The script called for Richard to enter a patient's room and explain that he was administering something to make them feel better. He then injected the potentially lethal drugs Pavulon and Anectine. The first drug paralyzed the patient, rendering him / her unable to call for help. The second drug induced a life threatening condition. When the patient was "code blue," our hero, Richard, would appear on the scene and, according to his script, rescue the stricken patient. However, of the 37 patients who would face the end of Richard's needle, 25 died. Richard proved to be an ineffectual hero.

The hospital became alarmed by the number of patients who seemed to be on the mend and then suddenly died, but the administrators did very little other than scratch their heads until the night of October 11, 1987.

That evening, Richard entered the room of a patient, Gerolamo Kucich, and told him, "I'm here to make you feel better." Richard proceeded to inject the drugs into Kucich, but this time, the patient sensed something was wrong and had the presence of mind to alert the nurse on duty. The nurse arrived and saved Mr. Kucich who provided a description of the notorious nurse. The description perfectly matched Richard Angelo.

The police searched Richard's locker which led to a search of his home where the lethal combination of drugs was found. Richard was questioned and at some point confessed, but his lawyer made sure the jury never heard that confession. His attorney claimed that Richard had multiple personalities, that one personality was unaware of the actions of the other personalities, thereby relieving him of responsibility. The judge did not allow this defense and the trial commenced.

In an emotional opening argument, John B. Collins, deputy bureau chief of the Suffolk County District Attorney's Homicide Bureau, addressed the jury, "Richard Angelo is the living embodiment of your worst nightmare.... To unsuspecting patients at the Good Samaritan special-care unit, Richard Angelo was a monster dressed in nurse's whites." Mr. Collins said. "He conducted uncontrolled experiments on unknowing, terribly vulnerable human beings for his stated purposes of improving his image and reputation."

The most damning testimony came from Richard's final victim, Gerolamo Kucich, who traveled from his home in Yugoslavia to testify. He had become sick while visiting relatives on Long Island, and that is how he came to be at the hospital that night.

In his testimony, Kucich described that night: The man asked him how he was feeling, Mr. Kucich said. "I say not bad," Mr. Kucich testified. "He opened up his coat and pulled out something that looked like a pen. Then he said, 'Now, you are going to feel much better.' " The man, he continued, then inserted a needle into his intravenous tubing. "At once, I feel like cold liquid running," he said. "I became dead. I couldn't move my muscles." Mr. Kucich testified that before he became completely paralyzed, he was able to press a buzzer to summon his nurse, Lauren Ball, who began resuscitating him.

In his confession, Richard said, "I wanted to create a situation where I would cause the patient to have some respiratory distress or some problem, and through my intervention or suggested intervention or whatever, come out looking like I knew what I was doing. I had no confidence in myself. I felt very inadequate."

Richard Angelo was found guilty. His 61-year sentence should prove an adequate amount of time for him to create a new, socially acceptable scenario.

1989: The Lonely Life of Oliver Petrovich

The reasons for murder are rarely simple and often not easily explained. Frequently, they are too complex for even the murderer to understand. This was the case for Oliver Petrovich. His lawyer said he killed his parents because his father threatened Oliver's relationship with his girlfriend; the prosecution said he did it because he wanted access to the million dollars the death of his parents would bring. Here is Oliver's story; you decide.

Svetozar (Peter) and Anna Petrovich came to this country from Yugoslavia with their four-year-old son Oliver in search of a better life. Until the third grade, Oliver was an average little boy. After that, things seemed to change. He was "a boy would grow up in virtual solitary confinement, a socially backward kid who became an alienated and disturbed young man with no friends and extremely bitter relations with his strict father and his weak mother…" His was a cold and bitter home life where there was just the word of his father to live by and the obedience of his weak mother who could never stand up to her husband. She was always caught between her husband who she both loved and feared and her son. She tried to keep peace in the home, but she too often failed, mostly because Peter was critical of everything his son said and did. Peter didn't like Oliver's choice of a job as a mechanic, and he especially didn't like his son's choice of girlfriends. Peter could not understand the fascination his son had with Africa American women. But Oliver found them exotic and more to his liking than white women.

Oliver's life took a definite upturn when he met Karlene Francis at the New Rochelle Mall. She needed money for something to eat and Oliver fell for her immediately. She was someone who needed him, and she saw him as strong and able to fulfill that need. This is the time when the happy ending should kick in, but there was just one problem. Karlene was black, and we know Oliver's father's feelings on that subject. There was just no way Oliver would ever be able to bring her home to Mom and Dad. The Sunday dinner might just end in bloodshed if they even got as far as dinner. Later on the stand in Oliver's murder trial, the psychologist Alan Klein suggested, "There were two all-important attachments in his life - his relationship with Miss Francis, and his relationship with his car," He also suggested that Karlene and Oliver's relationship was "almost mother-child"

But Oliver was not about to give up Karlene, his one chance at happiness. She dragged him up from his miserable existence and gave him the promise of a better life.

So, Oliver devised a plan to keep Karlene a secret from his father, but still keep her near. This is where the story gets a little odd. No, this is where it gets really odd. During the daytime, Karlene stayed in Oliver's bedroom closet, occasionally coming out to take a shower or get something to eat. We can only imagine the conversation when he brought up this idea. What in Karlene's life made her think this was a good idea? Can you imagine staying in that closet day in and day out, just waiting for either the love of your life to come home or for you to be caught in there and either arrested for breaking and entering or shot by Oliver's bigoted dad? That truly is love.

Oliver's mother eventually found out about Karlene and occasionally let her come downstairs where the women would talk while Peter and his father were both at work. We can only imagine those conversations between two women who had made very bad choices in the name of love. Both women probably did not see it, but they both were abused women. What was missing from each of their lives that they thought this life was all they could hope for? Did their conversation ever stray to planning their escape? I doubt it. It seems they both saw this life as the best they could hope for.

In the evenings, the lovers would go out. Karlene would climb out the bedroom window and crawl across the roof, meeting Oliver down the street. I guess love will conquer all, even two story houses and old roofs. When they arrived back at Oliver's house, Oliver would drop Karlene off at the corner and drive himself home. She would then crawl back in the window and spend the night with Oliver, returning the next morning to the closet, keeping herself out of Peter's way.

This was their life; each lived for the evenings when they could be together. Karlene literally lived for Oliver's presence. For a lonely, young man, this must have been paradise, a dream come true. The intrigue and drama of it all only added to the intensity. Oliver had gone from an isolated life to having his own genie in a bottle, there at his beck and call.

They wanted, though, more than anything, to have a normal life. For Oliver, the next step seemed obvious; he

130

had to kill his parents. For most of us, the next step would be to get his own place, but we are not Oliver, and the mind that cooked up the idea to keep his girlfriend in a closet would not immediately go toward anything conventional. He believed murdering his parents would give him and Karlene the freedom they desired. It would also give him the funds to do it. Oliver came up with a few plans, but none worked out. One was to fake a robbery in the basement of one of the apartment buildings that Peter owned. This plan was rejected because they could not get a gun with a silencer. The other plan was to club his parents to death and then set fire to their bodies. This, too, was rejected for reason's unknown. Perhaps as the planning got real, Oliver began to have cold feet.

All of this might have stayed in the planning stage, just two lovers fantasizing about how they could be free, if it not for two things. The first was a threat made by Peter that he would shoot Oliver if her saw him with a black woman. The second was Peter's mother's decision to tell Peter abut Karlene living in the bedroom closet. It isn't really clear what prompted this betrayal of Oliver's trust, but it is clear these two events were what forced Oliver's hand. If only Mom had kept her mouth shut; it might have saved them both.

On the day of the murders, there was a lot of agitation in Oliver's world, his car was giving him trouble, he couldn't fix his computer, and his parents had invited a family over for dinner whose daughter they wanted to hook up with Oliver. Because of this, Oliver could not go out with Karlene until late.

First Oliver attempted to strangle his mother. Perhaps this was Oliver's way to symbolically silence her. But strangulation is a pretty up close and personal way to kill. Possibly having his mother's face looking up at him while he killed her was too much for Oliver or maybe it was not as silent of a way as he had imagined. When that

132

failed, he shot her and then proceeded to the first floor master bedroom. At the sound of the gunshot that had killed his wife, Peter reached for the shotgun he kept behind the bedroom door, but it was not there. Oliver had already taken it. This was the first time, perhaps, when Oliver had bested his father and done something first. Oliver then stepped into the room and shot his father.

Karlene waited upstairs. After he was through, Oliver ran to a neighbor's house, acting (or maybe he wasn't acting) petrified, and claimed that he had returned home from a date and found the front door wide open. He said he was afraid to go inside and asked that the neighbor call the police. Inconsistencies in Oliver's story made him the center of the police's attention, and he was arrested.

After his arrest, Oliver did not immediately confess. Karlene later would testify that the police tricked her into convincing Oliver to confess. She claimed they told her that if he confessed he would not go to jail but to a mental hospital. This shows how naïve both were. They truly believed that they would get to go home together if they just told the truth. Believing this, Karlene went in and told Oliver that she knew he killed his parents, but if he confessed he could go to a hospital rather than to jail and would soon go home with her.

So, Oliver confessed. What followed was a 17-page confession. In it we can hear the voice of a man who was in a "state of panic" in "warfare between his heart and his mind." He said, "I thought I was doing the right thing. Now I know I didn't do the right thing…If I didn't kill my parents, I would be sitting with Angel (Karlene) now in my room."

This confession became the subject of a pre-trial motion by Oliver's attorney, Nicholas Marino, who declared that the confession should be excluded because it was obtained by "psychological coercion." Karlene testified, against her own attorney's advice, "I was told I was the only person who could help him and if I told them exactly what happened they promised me he wouldn't go to jail, that he would go to a psychiatric hospital." This promise was what made Karlene go in to encourage Oliver to confess.

Marino asked her on the stand, "Based on your relationship with Oliver, would he do what you asked him to do?"

"Yes," Frances replied, "to make me happy."

On the last day of this hearing, Oliver wept at the mere mention of Karlene's name. The judge reserved his decision.

As the trial began, Olive sat in the courtroom day after day waiting for it all to be over so he could go home and begin their lives together. He had no doubt that Karlene would stand by his side; look at what she had already done to be with him. She loved him enough to testify for him and wait for him should he have to go to jail. We can imagine he was sure and that was what kept him hopeful that she would never testify against him.

Oliver's love and fascination with her was evident to all by his courtroom behavior. He blew her kisses and wrote notes to her on a yellow legal pad. She mouthed to him that she was looking for engagement rings.

But, when it came time for her to testify, she refused by invoking her constitutional rights to not incriminate herself. Oliver was infuriated, he stood up and yelled, "My girlfriend was just here. The judge threw her out... I've got one witness and she gets thrown out."

Mr. Marino believed, "She is the only person living... who can give first-hand testimony as to what happened in that house over all those months. That's so pivotal to my client's defense and we've been denied that."

Nicholas Marino, Oliver's lawyer, had to make sure that the jury saw him as a possessed young man, obsessed and controlled by the love he had for Karlene and how fearful he was of his father's bigoted rage against her. Oliver's outburst only helped his case. The prosecution saw Oliver's outburst as calculated.

As for the mental state of Oliver, the experts weighed in on that by saying that Oliver appreciated the consequences of his actions. He did this to be free with the money of his father in his pocket.

Before the closing arguments began, Oliver insisted that the jury not be given the option of manslaughter, just murder. This was done against his lawyers wishes. Many believed that this was a shrewd plot of Oliver's. If the jury was even a bit unsure, it might be easier to convict him of the lesser charge. But if all they had to choose from was 2nd degree murder, they might not convict at all. A calculated move? Perhaps, but one that didn't work. The prosecution saw it as "a deliberate, calculated attempt by this defendant to try to bamboozle the jury into thinking he's insane."

After nine hours of deliberations, the jury came back with a verdict of guilty of 2nd degree murder. "The question that we wrestled with for the bulk of our session is if he knew and appreciated the consequences of his actions," said juror Phil Chin of Massapequa Park. "There was strong discussion of whether he knew it was wrong . . . when he pulled the trigger the first time and then the second time." Another juror said, ""There was no medium between guilty and not guilty by reason of mental disease or defect," juror Ronald Mancuso of Hicksville said outside the courthouse after the verdict. "We had no alternative but to come to the verdict of guilty"

Oliver looked out of the window and did not seem to even hear the verdict. He received a sentence of 50 years to life... all that time without Angel.

1989 Who Called Kelly? The Murder of Kelly Ann Tinyes

On March 3, 1989, Kelly Ann Tinyes went missing after walking into a neighbor's house on Horton Avenue in Valley Stream. She was never seen alive again. The murder of this young girl was soon solved, but the echoes of that day can still be heard on this Long Island street.

After school on the afternoon of the murder, Steve Bataan and Glen McMahon went to classmate John Jay Golub's home to smoke pot and play Nintendo. Also at home was John Jay's 21-year-old brother Robert. The story told was that John Jay left the room about three times, once to make a phone call. The three friends left about an hour later and played basketball at a local school, leaving only Robert Golub home.

As for Kelly Ann, she was babysitting for her younger brother, Richard. He answered the phone about

2:00 and told Kelly, "It's for you, it's John" (meaning John Golub). About 2:15, she told Richard that she was going to visit a friend who lived next to the Golub's. She could not say that she was going to the Golub's because she was forbidden to go there. John Jay was seen as a bully in that neighborhood, often beating up much younger kids. Kelly Ann's parents didn't want her to associate with someone that violent.

Six-year-old Jimmy Walsh, a neighbor, later told police that he had seen John Jay open the door and let Kelly Ann into his house. That is the last time she was seen alive.

After a while, Kelly's brother grew concerned and called the Golub home, but there was no answer. He then went to the Golub door and knocked numerous times with still no response.

When Mrs. Tinyes arrived home, she went to the Golub house to see if John or his brother had seen Kelly, but was told no. When Mr. Tinyes arrived home at about 6 p.m., he called all of Kelly's friends and trolled the neighborhood, the local malls, parks and playgrounds. When he arrived home without Kelly, Mrs. Tinyes called the police and reported her daughter missing. She also indicated to the police, though, that it was possible Kelly had left on her own accord. The next morning, Mrs. Golub went from house to house demanding to know what people had seen the previous day.

The day after Kelly went missing, the police requested to search the Golub's home. Mrs. Golub spoke to her husband on the phone, and he demanded that the search wait until he arrived home. When the police finally got access to the Golub house, they were shocked to see the condition. All the rooms were loaded with trash and clothes. In the kitchen, counters, and sink were piled with dirty dishes. Both the master bedroom and the bath did not look like anyone could use them as they were filled with clothes and trash. Even the bath tub was filled with clothing. As the police went from room to room, they saw the same kind of disarray throughout. The police could not imagine anyone actually living there.

Once Mr. Golub arrived, the search began in earnest. One of the detectives searched the basement. He opened a closet that was blocked by clothing, bottles and other debris. In the closet was a sleeping bag with a foot sticking out. Kelly had been found. In a nearby briefcase, were the bloody clothes Kelly had worn.

John's story to the police was that he and his friends played Nintendo in the living room until 3:45. No one came to the house. While the police were questioning him at his house, John was anxious to reach his friend Steve Bataan. After the police interview, John and his uncle went to Steven's house. When he reached his home, John was "irritable and nervous" and demanded to see Steve. He was told that Bataan was already at the police station. John did not believe this and yelled, "Tell them we were playing Nintendo," not the coolest of moves if he wanted the police to dismiss him as a subject.

At 5 p.m., Robert was brought to the police station and told the police that he had been home all afternoon but did not see or hear anyone except his brother and his brother's friends. During this time, Golub gave a bite impression. The police thought he appeared to have no motive for the crime, and he also passed a lie detector test. For these reasons after numerous hours of questioning, Robert was released.

This began the decade's long tension on Horton Avenue. The neighbors were frustrated that Golub was not under the arrest. Police even had to rescue him from a mob that followed him into a supermarket calling, "Murderer, Murderer."

Three weeks later, after an indictment from a Grand

Jury, Robert Golub voluntarily surrendered and was

officially indicted for 2nd degree murder in the death of

Kelly Ann Tinyes. Det. Wayne Seay told reporters that the

evidence was "substantial and significant." and that John Jr.

was no longer an official suspect, although the

investigation was ongoing and that could change.

Robert plead not-guilty and his lawyer indicated

that Robert did not show remorse because he had nothing to

be remorseful about. The medical examiner captivated the

whole courtroom when he gave an injury by injury

description of what happened to Kelly Anne. Sometime

between noon and 6 p.m. on the day she went missing, she

was first hit in the mouth and around the face area with a

blunt object until she was unconscious. After that, she was

strangled, and at some point she was stomped on the neck.

After this brutal assault, her clothes were removed, her

body sliced with, perhaps, a piece of mirror or glass and her sexual organs were maimed. This went on for at least 20 minutes.

The trial was painful for all parties. The medical examiner, Dr. Arlene Cohen, testified to the various injuries to Kelly's body; she testified that Kelly had tufts of hair ripped from her head and she was smeared with her own blood. She had been mutilated to the point of making an autopsy very difficult. Robert Golub had very little reaction to this, but Kelly's mother cried throughout. During some of the testimony, there were outburst from the audience toward the Golubs.

Golub was found guilty after the jury deliberated only one day. He was sentenced to 25 years to life. He is, though, eligible for parole. The court room erupted in cries from the friends and family of the victim. These people screamed at the Golubs and some had to be forcibly removed from the court.

After the trial, the Tinyes families continued to ask the District Attorney to reopen the case and look for evidence that John Jr. was also involved in the killing. Their confidence was supported by the story of a child who claimed to see through a basement window the murder of Kelly. She claimed that the windows were very dirty, but she thought she saw two people with Kelly. The police discounted this because of the age of the child.

Starting after the verdict, the police received numerous calls that brought them back to Horton Road. Victoria Tinyes was charged with driving her car at Elizabeth Golub while John Golub was arrested and accused of driving his car into Richard Golub's truck. These were just two of the dozens of call the police received over those years after the verdict.

The Tinyes family even sued the Golubs for 600 million dollars claiming they were negligent parents, failing to watch their children. This suit went nowhere.

Each felt the other should move, but for a long time each said they could not afford to move. In 2009, the Golubs finally moved.

Twenty-five years later, in a failed bid to receive parole, Robert confessed to killing Kelly Ann, but claimed it was all some tragic accident brought on by his use of anabolic steroids. "I had come out of my room and I was running down the stairs and I ran into Kelly on the stairs. She fell down the stairs. She became unconscious. I panicked. I didn't call for assistance.... Instead of calling somebody for help, I took her by the ankle and pulled her through the house, and her jacket, and her shirt, and everything rode up; when I read she had suffocated, I believe that's what happened. She was unconscious from the time she hit the bottom of the stairs. She never regained consciousness, at all."

Kelly's father, though, did not get any satisfaction out of the confession, "Now he's trying to say he's sorry 25 years later. It's out of control…It doesn't bring any

justice…. all he is trying to do is get out of jail."

1993 A Fool for a Client: The Crimes and Trial of Colin Ferguson

Colin Ferguson stepped onto the 5:31 train out of Penn Station on December 7, 1993; when the train stopped in Garden City, the lives of 25 people and those they loved would never be the same.

Colin Ferguson was born in Kingston, Jamaica, to a wealthy pharmacist, considered one of the most important people in Jamaica. He had four brothers and grew up in a 2-story house with a nanny and housekeeper. He graduated in the top one-third of his high school class. His teachers and classmates considered him a well-rounded kid. This view of Colin would later surprise those who saw him on the train that night.

When Colin was 20, his father died in a car crash, and his mother died of cancer soon after. The death of his father destroyed the family's financial security and deeply disturbed Colin. When Colin moved to the US a few years later on a visitor's visa, he was deeply troubled by what he saw as severe racism and was disheartened that the only work he could find was unskilled. In 1986, he married Audrey Warren, possibly to qualify for permanent resident status.

After marrying, he and Audrey moved to Long Island where the police were called to their home on many occasions to investigate reports of domestic violence. That happy child growing up in Jamaica had become a very angry man. In 1988, Audrey divorced Colin. She said that he was too aggressive, and they had different views on the world. This divorce was a crushing blow to Colin's ego.

The next year, while at work, Colin slipped off a stool, hurting his head, neck, and back. After filing for Workman's Compensation, he enrolled in Nassau County Community College where he was on the Dean's List three times. But he left school when he got overly aggressive during a confrontation with an instructor.

In 1990, Colin transferred to Adelphi University and continued with his belligerent stance on race relations. He ranted about having to coexist with whites and called for a violent revolution. Everyone he encountered he accused of behaving in a racist manner toward him, once accusing a white co-ed of yelling racial slurs at him when he asked her for a school assignment. The university investigated and found no basis for Ferguson's allegations.

A particularly disturbing event happened at a symposium where a woman was relating her experiences in South Africa. Ferguson yelled "Kill everybody white! We should be talking about the revolution in South Africa and how to get rid of white people." Colin then accused the police of racism and brutality.

This side of Colin was masked when he later rented a room in Flatbush. His neighbors said he was polite and well-dressed; basically, he was well liked in the neighborhood. But Colin's underlying hatred began to reemerge when he remarked to his landlord, "I'm such a great person. There must be only one thing holding me back. It must be white people."

In 1992, his ex-wife Audrey accused him of prying open the trunk of her car. Around the same time, he was accused of stalking and harassing a white woman after she tried to sit next to him on a subway train. He was subdued by the police and could be heard screaming, "Brothers, come help me!"

In September of 1992, Colin's Workmen's Comp case was finally settled; he received $26, 250. The next year, Colin demanded his case be re-opened because he was still in pain and wanted more money. Colin's female attorney said he made her very uncomfortable after he threatened the law firm. She always had another lawyer present during meetings with Colin. The case was reopened, immediately rejected and Colin was put on a list of dangerous people at the law firm.

In April of 1993, Colin moved to California. The only work he could find was a job at a car wash. This was when he purchased a Ruger P-89 9 mm hand gun. After being robbed by two black men, he started carrying the gun at all times. Colin moved back to NYC the next month telling people he didn't like having to compete for work with immigrants and Hispanics. His landlord said Colin seemed to be more unstable and constantly talked about the blacks rising up to defeat their oppressors.

On December 7, 1993, Colin Ferguson purchased a Long Island Rail Road ticket at Pennsylvania Station and boarded the third car on the eastbound 5:33 train to Hicksville. He carried the handgun he had purchased in

California and 160 rounds of ammunition. There were 80 other passengers on board the train.

As they were pulling into the Merillion Avenue station, Colin walked down the aisle of the car shooting methodically from right to left and back again. Many passengers tried hiding under their seats. As Colin shot each victim, he said, "I'm going to get you."

Some of the passengers escaped to other cars while some forced open the door and fled to the station. The engineer did not open the car doors because two of the cars had not yet reached the platform, so one conductor squeezed through a window and opened the doors from the outside.

When Colin stopped briefly to reload, someone yelled, "Grab him" and Michael O'Connor, Kevin Blum, and Mark McEntee pinned Colin to the nearest seat while others held his arms and legs. Colin was heard saying "Oh,

God, what did I do? What did I do? I deserve whatever I get." In the back of the police car, all that remorse was gone and would never appear again.

When he was searched, small slips of paper were found jammed in his pocket saying, "Reason for this—racism by Caucasian and Uncle Tom Negroes." He also wrote about his anger toward the woman in his previous subway incident, the Workers Comp Board, all Asians, Governor Cuomo, and the civil rights leaders. He, also, had in his possession the names and telephone numbers of the NY Lt. Governor, the Attorney General, the NY law firm he had previously hired, and "the corrupt black attorney who refused to help me and stole my car." All these people he blamed for sabotaging his life, and he had chosen the LIRR as the site for his revenge.

Initially, Ferguson hired attorneys William Kunstler and Ronald Kuby who wanted to use a "black rage" defense, in effect saying that years of racism caused Colin

Ferguson to snap on the train that night. '"It is necessary to see the torment he was going through as a racial victim to see what drove him to this action," said Ronald Kuby" …'
"This holds the white community responsible in part for the fruits of racism. It is not an excuse for black men to commit crimes. It is a defense which will allow a man who was driven insane by white injustice to show that he was insane when he committed this crime," he said. Black news commentators felt the defense was patronizing and racist.

But, Colin Ferguson was now proclaiming he was actually innocent and that a white man had stolen his gun while he slept on the train and committed the crimes. He fired his lawyers and asked to defend himself. Having been found sane, Ferguson had that right, and so the judge allowed it, having Ronald Kuby stay on to aid Ferguson.

Some of Ferguson's initial moves as his own attorney were less than professional. First, he wrote motions about the bad food in jail. Next, he wanted to subpoena President Clinton and Governor Cuomo. When questioning potential jurors, he asked questions like "what are your ambitions?" and "raise your hand if you are a hockey fan." He also indicated that the reason there were 92 indictments against him was that the year was 1992. You could sense that if it weren't unprofessional, the judge and prosecutor would be rolling their eyes at the antics of the defendant.

One of the first victims to testify was survivor Elizabeth Avilis, who testified that she saw Ferguson "pump bullets into commuters" as he shot from left to right. As she huddled on the floor, he shot her in the back. But even as she very clearly told the jury that she saw him shoot the people on the train that night, his response was "Is it your testimony that you saw no one shot?" he inquired. "I saw you shooting everyone on the train, okay?" eyewitness Aviles replied angrily. The indignity of being shot by Ferguson and then having to face him in the

157

courtroom and have him try to trick the victims into saying his didn't shoot them must have been almost unbearable. And even though witness after witness pointed at Ferguson and said "I saw you shoot those people," Ferguson still went on *Larry King Live* and said, "Very few witnesses were able to point a finger at me."

When it came time for Ferguson to put up his defense, the excuses started to mount. He had claimed on *The Today Show* that he had a ballistics expert, handwriting expert, and two eye witnesses all set up to testify for him. But now he claimed that witnesses were afraid to come forward for fear for their lives. Next, he claimed that the paperwork he had in a folder had fallen and then gotten all mixed up so he couldn't follow it anymore. He also claimed that he needed more time to prepare his defense since the curfew restrictions in the prison were so restrictive. He came just short of saying his dog ate his defense.

At this the judge pointed out that Mr. Ferguson had the time to go on *The Today Show* and *Larry King*, he should have the time to prepare a defense. At this point the judge, who had displayed infinite patience with Ferguson up to that point, grew agitated. But Ferguson, who appeared to love the sound of his own voice and was seeing his 15 minutes of fame slipping away, claimed that the Jewish Defense League was planning to have him killed if he was convicted. In addition, the murder of Jeffrey Dahmer in prison the previous year was "set up as a prelude against me."

Without his extensions, Ferguson rested his case. In his closing argument, Ferguson continued to claim that all the witnesses were conspiring with the prosecution and lying about him. The jury took little time in finding Ferguson guilty; he listened to the verdict stone-faced. Then during to the penalty phase, it took three days for the defense and prosecution to set out their pleas.

The first day of the penalty phase, Ferguson spent three hours ranting about the media, prosecution, judge and jury: "John the Baptist lived in the wilderness, a humble man, and he was put into prison for no reason. He was beheaded by a criminal justice system similar to this." Many survivors left during his tirade. Carolyn McCarthy, whose husband had been killed and son gravely injured, said "Hopefully, today will be the last of Colin Ferguson."

The second day the victims and their families got their chance to tell Ferguson and the court the impact that day in the LIRR had on their lives. Some even brought Ferguson's legal advisor to tears.

Colin Ferguson was found guilty in the attempted murder of those injured that night and murder for those killed. He received over 315 years in prison and will be eligible for parole in the year 2309.

The judge's final words to Ferguson were, "What could be more cowardly than to enter a train filled with unsuspecting homebound commuters and systematically shoot them all point blank range."

References

Abbott, G. (n.a.). *Amazing True Stories of Execution*. Retrieved from Murderpedia: murderpedia.org/female.c./c/creighton-mary-frances.htm

AP. (1988, November 19). Jury Fins L.I. Man Guilty of Strangling of Wife. *New York Times*.

Bassent, A. (1989, Oct. 12). A Courtroom Shocker Petrovich: Forget lesser charge. *Newsday*, p. 5.

Bassent, A. (1989, 10 11). Experts say Petrovich not Insane. *Newsday*, p. 23.

Bassent, A. (1989, March 16). Her Lover's Confession Girlfriend: I persuaded Petrovich to admit killings. *Newsday*, p. 5.

Baum, G. (1985, November 1). Gold Coasts "Perfect Mystery". *Newsday*.

Bessent, A. (1989, Oct. 13). Petrovich Guilty of Killing Parents Jury: No Alternative but Murder Verdict. *Newsday*, p. 5.

Bessent, A. (1989, Oct. 4). Petrovich Upset That Girlfriend Won't Testify. *Newsday*.

Biography.com. (2015). *Ronald DeFeo*. Retrieved from Biography: www.biography.com/people/ronald-defeo-580972

Blanco, J. (n.a.). *Mary Frances Creighton*. Retrieved from Murderpedia: mruderpedia.org/femail.c./c/creighton-mary-francis.htm

Boccella, K. (1987, December 27). Wide Ranging Search for Missing Woman. *Newsday*.

Bovsun, M. (2008, April 16). The Long Island Borgia. *The Daily News*.

Bresking, D. (1984, November 22). *Rolling Stone*.

Bruchey, S. (2006, April 24). A "Horror" Revisted. *Newsday*.

Colin Ferguson. (n.a.). Retrieved from Murderpedia: http://murderpedia.org/male.F/f/ferguson-colin.htm

Crocker, B. (2011, March 13). *What really happened to Starr Faithfull?* Retrieved from Crasstalk: crasstalk.com/2011/03/2011/what-really-happened-to-starr-faithfull

Demoretcky, T. a. (1988, January 12). Cops: Solomon admits Killing wiife, charged in murder. *Newsday*.

Dorman, M. (1998, May 29). A Slaying in high sciety. *Newsday*.

Dorman, M. (1998, June 1). Long Island: Our Story- Held for Ransom. *Newsday*.

Dorning, M. (1992, October 5). The good life gone bad: Murder in high society. *Chicago Tribune*.

Edginton, J. (Director). (2006). *First Person Killers: Ronald DeFeo* [Motion Picture].

Families and both victim and killer remain on same street 20 years after teen slaying. (2008, March 27). Retrieved from FoxNews: www.foxnews.com

Flanagan Brosky, K. (2013, January 13). *The Wickham Murders of 1854.* Retrieved from Huntington Patch: patch.com/new-york/huntington/bp-the-wickham-murders-of-1854

Geordie, G. (1994, April 17). Black rage plea by train killer. *The London Times*.

Gibson, I. (1915, August 10). The Case of Little Jack De Saulles. *The Pittseburgh Press.*

Goldberg, N. (1989, January 2). The Night They Found Lisa Solomon's Body. *Newsday.*

Goldstein, M. (1956, July 4). 1956: A Crime Without End. *Newsday.*

Goodman, J. (1990). *The Passing of Starr Faithfull.* Kent, OH: Kent State University Press.

Gribbon, M. (n.d.). *A Lifetime in a month.* Retrieved from The Malefactor's Register: http://malefactorsregister.com/wp/?p=314

Gutis, P. (1989, October 20). Former patient points to nurse in murder trail. *The New York Times.*

Hester, J. (1998, December 11th). Counsel for the defense Colin Ferguson goes to trial. *New York Daily News.*

Holland, E. (2013, September 26). *Sin and Scandal: The De Saulles Murder Case.* Retrieved from Edwardian Promenade: http://www.edwardianpromenade.com/crime/sin-and-scandal-the-de-saulles-murder-case/

Keeler, B. (1986, March 19). DeFeo's New Story. *Newsday.*

Ketcham, D. (1988, November 20). Drama at the Solomon Trial. *New York Ties.*

Kindall, J. (1989, April 12). A murder for prime time. *Newsday.*

Kleiman, D. (1986, September 14). Murder on Long Island. *New York Times Magazine.*

Krajicek, D. (1989, February 18). A Secret turned Deadly. *Daily News.*

Leavitt, J. (1996). *Typhoid Mary: Captive to the piblic's health.* Boston: Beacon Press.

Leavitt, J. (2004, October 12). *Typhoid Mary: Villian or Victim.* Retrieved from Nova: www.pbs.org/wgbh/nova/body/typhoid-mary-villian-or-victim.html

Leung, R. (2004, March 30). *Forever changed.* Retrieved from 48 Hours: www.cbsnews.com/news/forever-changed/

Long Island Genealogy. (n.d.). *Huntington's Horrible Tar Town Murder.* Retrieved from Long Island Genealogy: http://longislandgenealogy.com/tar.html

Lowe, E. (1998, June 21). Long Island: Our Story. *Newsday.*

Lyall, S. (1990, March 1). Blood Tests Link Golub to Crime Scene. *New York Times.*

Lyall, S. (1990, February 27). Slain Girl's Bloody Clothing Displayed by Expert at Trial. *The New York Times.*

M., G. (n.a.). *They Called Her Borgia.* Retrieved from Murderpedia: murderpedia.org/female.c./c/creighton-mary-frances.htm

Maier, T. (1986, December 9). The Jailhouse Snithes. *Newsday.*

Martino, M. (2009, March 5). The Last Call. *Long Island Press.*

McQuiston, J. (1995, February 16). Abrupt end to defense in rail case. *New York Times.*

Milton, P. (1989, October 12). Man guilty of Killing mother and father. *The Gazzette.*

Milton, P. (1995, March 23). Railroad slayer gets life in prison. *York Daily Record.*

Montatdo, C. (n.d.). *Profile of serial killer Richard Angelo.* Retrieved from About.com: crime.about.com/od/serial/richardangelo.htm

Mrs. Florence Carman arrested and help on charges of murder. (1914, July 9). Retrieved from Meriden Weekly Republican: https://news.google.com/newspapers?nid=2515&dat=1 9140709&id=FHxHAAAAIBAJ&sjid=gf4MAAAAIBAJ&pg= 1764,5810581&hl=en

Murphy, B. (2013, December 11). Golub's Admission 25 Years later he tells board he killed Kelly Ann. *Newsday.*

n.a. (1887, Oct. 4). *An Islap Murder Mystery.* Retrieved from Victorian Criminology: victoriancriminology.blogspot.com

n.a. (1887, Oct. 14). *New York Times,Slain by Own Son.* Retrieved from Victorian Criminology: victoriancriminology.blogspot.com

n.a. (1917, August 5). INSANITY DEFENCE PLANNED TO SAVE MRS DE SAULLES. *New York Times.*

n.a. (1989). *A Historical Overview of the Office of the Suffolk County Sheriff and His Department.* n.a.: n.a.

n.a. (1990, March 4). The Search for Justice: one good reason to reopen Tinyes case. *Newsday.*

n.a. (2008). *America's Most Famous Haunted House Controversey.* Retrieved from AmityFiles.com: www.amityfile.com/haunting.htm

n.a. (2009, March 27). *Murder Revisited.* Retrieved from The Unknown History of Misandry:

http://unknownmisandry.blogspot.com/2011/09/mary-creighton-new-jersey-serial-killer.html

n.a. (2011, September 22). *Mary Crieghton, New Jersey Serial Killer*. Retrieved from The Unknown History of Misandry: http://unknownmisandry.blogspot.com/2011/09/mary-creighton-new-jersey-serial-killer.html

Newton, M. (n.d.). *An encyclopedia of modern serial killers-hunting humans.* Retrieved from Murderpedia: http://murderpedia.org/male.A/a/angelo-richard.htm

Nieves, E. (1998, May 31). *What happened on Horton Road.* Retrieved from NYTimes: www.nytimes.com

Ochs, R. (1998, April 13). Long Island: Our Story- Dinner with Typhoid Mary. *Newsday.*

O'Neill, J., & Brooks, S. (1990, October 14). Nashua owner slain by wife on LI. *Newsday.*

Paris, L. (2011, June 27). *True crime on the North Fork: The Wickham axe murders.* Retrieved from 27eat.com: http://www.27east.com/news/article.cfm/General-Interest/388814/True-Crime-On-The-North-Fork-The-Wickham-Axe-Murders/start/2

Perlman S. & Scovel, J. (1990, March 13). Last Minutes of Kelly Tinyes' Life: doctor details lengthy attack. *Newsday.*

Perlman, S. &. (1987, September 15). The House of Hell. *Newsday.*

Perlman, S. (1987, September 17). Pierson's role in slaying probed. *Newsday.*

Perlman, S. (1988, January 20). Cheryly Pierson gets out. *Newsday.*

Perlman, S. (1988, January 10). Mother's Memory of Lisa Solomon. *Newsday*.

Perlman, S. (1989, August 18). Bite Marks Bombshell: Tinyes wounds were inflicted by Golub. *Newsday*.

Perlman, S. (1989, August 18). Bite-Marks Bombshell: Prosecutor- Tinyes' wound were inflicted by Golub. *Newsday*.

Perlman, S. (1989, March 19). Her Lover's Confession Girlfriend: I persuaded Petrovich to admit killings. *Newsday*.

Perlman, S. (1989, November 3). Mrs. Golub: Okd search ina daze. *Newday*.

Perlman, S. (1989, January 13). Suspected from the First Probe's Focus always on Matthew Solomon, police say. *Newsday*.

Perlman, S. (1990, June 2). 25 Yesrs to ife: Golub says he's innocent, attacks court system. *Newsday*.

Perlman, S. S. (1990, April 4). The Verdict on Golub: Guilty jury reqaches decision in less than 8 hours. *Newsday*.

Philibert-Ortega, G. (2013, June 6). *Investigating the murder mystery of Louis Bailey with newspapers*. Retrieved from Genealogy Bank: http://blog.genealogybank.com/investigating-the-murder-mystery-of-louise-bailey-with-newspapers.html

Porter, D. (2001). *Hollywood's Silent Closet*. Staten Island, NY: Porter & Prince Corp.

Primetime. (n.a.). *Amityville Horror: Horror or Hoax*. Retrieved from ABC News: www.abcnews.go.com/Primetime/story?id=132035

Quinttner, J. (1987, October 6). Pierson tale is marketable commodity. *Newsday*.

Ricky Kasso. (n.d.). Retrieved from Murderpedia: www.murderpedia.org/malek/k/kass-ricky.htm

Roseberg, J. (n.d.). *Typhoid Mary*. Retrieved from About.Com: www.history1900s.about.com/od/1900s/a/typhoidmary.htm

Rosen, M. (1994, June 6). An Echo of Murder. *Newsday*.

Rothchild, R. (2001, April 1). *Tar and Feathering of Charles Kelsey*. Retrieved from Delayed Reaction Lounge: http://delayedreactionlounge.blogspot.com/2011/04/paranormal-pub-tar-feather.html

Ruppel, L. (1988, January 11). People Don't Know: Matthew Solomon tells of last night with slain wife. *Newsday*.

Saslow, L. (1991). *For My Angel*. New York: Guild America Books.

Schmitt, E. (1989, March 4). Neighbor is Charged in Death of 13-year-old. *New York Times*.

Schulman, B. (2006, September 24). *Ann Woodward*. Retrieved from Signs of Charring or Melting: www.signsofcharring.blogspot.com/2006/09/ann-woodward-they-were-ideally-suited.html

Segrave, K. (2009). *Parricide in the United States, 1840-1899*. Jefferson: McFarland & Company, Inc.

Serial Killer Couple, The Lonely Hearts Killers, The Honeymoon Killers. (n.d.). Retrieved from Murderpedia: http://murderpedia.org/female.B/b/beck-martha.htm

Sherwood, D. a. (2007, July 22). The Real Lonely Hearts Kills. *Sunday Mirror*.

Simpson, L. (2016, January 10). *Local Girl Loses Election*. Retrieved from Springfield News: http://www.sprinfieldnews.com

Tanaka, R. (2011, December 24). *The Scandalously Fabulous Joan Sawyer*. Retrieved from The Killing of John L. de Saulles: http://jackdesaulles.blogspot.com/

The dictaphone murder trail of 1914: a mystery in pictures. (1914, July 16). Retrieved from The Bowery Boys: http://www.boweryboyshistory.com/2014/07/the-dictophone-murder-trial-of-1914.html

The Mysterious Death of Starr FaithfullRevealsa Boston Mayor's Sordid Secret. (2014). Retrieved from New England Historical Society: http://www.newenglandhistoricalsociety.com/the-mysterious-death-of-starr-faithfull-reveals-a-boston-mayors-sordid-secret/

The Sordid Affair. (1994). In *Crimes and Punishment: The Illustrated Crime Encyclopedia* (pp. 121-124). Westport, Conn.: H. S. Stuttman Inc. Publishers.

The strange death of Lulu Bailey. (2013, April 19). Retrieved from Patos Papa: https://patospapa.wordpress.com/2013/04/23/the-strange-death-of-lulu-bailey-part-2/

Vitello, P. (1989, Oct. 6). Only Victims in Oliver's War. *Newsday*.

Yardley, J. (1999, May 8). Heir to a fortune and to tragedy, suicide ends the life of a wealthy and haunted man. *The New York Times*.

56700774R00096

Made in the USA
Middletown, DE
27 July 2019